# SOCIOLOGICAL SNAPSHOTS

TITLES OF RELATED INTEREST FROM PINE FORGE PRESS

*Crime and Everyday Life: Insight and Implication for Society*, 2nd Edition by Marcus Felson

*Exploring Social Issues Using SPSS® for Windows*™ by Joseph F. Healey, Earl Babbie, and Fred Halley

*Race, Ethnicity, Gender, and Class: The Sociology of Group Conflict and Change*, 2nd Edition by Joseph F. Healey

*Illuminating Social Life: Classical and Contemporary Theory Revisited* by Peter Kivsito

*Key Ideas in Sociology* by Peter Kivisto

*Sociology: Exploring the Architecture of Everyday Life*, 2nd Edition by David Newman

*Sociology: Exploring the Architecture of Everyday Life, (Readings)* 2nd Edition by David Newman

*The McDonalidization of Society, Revised Edition* by George Ritzer

*Second Thoughts: Seeing Conventional Wisdom Through the Sociological Eye* by Janet M. Ruane and Karen A. Cerulo

*Shifts in the Social Contract: Understanding Change in American Society* by Beth A. Rubin

# SOCIOLOGICAL SNAPSHOTS

## Seeing Social Structure and Change in Everyday Life

**JACK LEVIN**
*Northeastern University*

PINE FORGE PRESS
*Thousand Oaks, California* ▪ *London* ▪ *New Delhi*

Copyright © 1999 by Pine Forge Press

All rights reserved. No part of this book may be reproduced or utilized in any form or by any means, electronic or mechanical, including photocopying, recording, or by any information storage and retrieval system, without permission in writing from the publisher.

*For information:*

Pine Forge Press
A Sage Publications Company
2455 Teller Road
Thousand Oaks, California 91320
E-mail. sales@pfp.sagepub.com

SAGE Publications Ltd.
6 Bonhill Street
London EC2A 4PU
United Kingdom

SAGE Publications India Pvt. Ltd.
M-32 Market
Greater Kailash I
New Delhi 110 048 India

*Printed in the United States of America*

1  2  3  4  5  6  7  05  04  03  02  01  00  99

**Library of Congress Cataloging-in-Publication Data**

Levin, Jack, 1941–
  Sociological snapshots 3: Seeing social structure and change in everyday life / Jack Levin.
    p.   cm.
  Includes bibliographical references and index.
  ISBN 0-7619-8592-1 (pbk.: acid-free paper)
  1. Sociology. 2. Social change. 3. Social structure—United States. 4. United States—Social conditions—1980- I. Title. II. Title: Sociological snapshots three
HM51 .L3587 1998
301—ddc21                                                           98-9081

*Production Manager:* Windy Just
*Production Editor:* Wendy Westgate
*Interior Designer:* Lisa S. Mirski
*Typesetter:* Christina M. Hill
*Cover Designer:* Ravi Balasuriya
*Visual Essays by* Shelley Kowalski

# Contents

**PREFACE / ix**

**THE SOCIOLOGICAL EYE** / 1

INTRODUCTION / 3
Just How Powerful Is a Role? / 10
Better Late Than Never / 12
Heartburn and Modern Times / 16
FOCUS: *Suggestions for Further Reading* / 18
DEVELOPING IDEAS: *About Social Structure* / 20

**PART ONE** **Culture / 23**

INTRODUCTION / 25
The Immaculate Americans / 30
Baby Boomers / 33
The Demise of Bystander Apathy / 37
We Are in the Midst of a Cultural Revolution / 41
Elevator Culture / 44
FOCUS: *Suggestions for Further Reading* / 46
DEVELOPING IDEAS: *About Culture* / 47

**PART TWO** **Socialization / 51**

INTRODUCTION / 53
Teaching Students They Are Not
   at the Center of the Universe
   (with Wilfred Holton) / 57
Confessions of a Soap Opera Addict / 61
Violence in City Schools
   (with Heather Beth Johnson) / 65
Sticks and Stones May Break . . . / 67

Adult Socialization Can Be Murder / 70
FOCUS: *Suggestions for Further Reading* / 72
DEVELOPING IDEAS: *About Socialization* / 75

## PART THREE — The Group Experience / 79

INTRODUCTION / 81

College Fraternities: A Counteracting Force on Campus / 84
The Appeal of Cults / 86
Reunion, American Style / 89
Children of the Organization Men / 92
FOCUS: *Suggestions for Further Reading* / 95
DEVELOPING IDEAS: *About the Group Experience* / 96

## PART FOUR — Institutions / 99

INTRODUCTION / 101

Who's Minding the Kids? / 104
Let the System Do It! / 106
Americans Are Moving to the Margins of Society / 108
Dirty Work / 111
FOCUS: *Suggestions for Further Reading* / 114
DEVELOPING IDEAS: *About Institutions* / 115

## PART FIVE — Deviance / 119

INTRODUCTION / 121

Fat Chance in a Slim World / 125
You Must Get Ill First; Then You Recover / 129
Is the Death Penalty Only a Vehicle for Revenge? / 131
Animal Cruelty and Human Violence (with Arnold Arluke) / 135
America's Youngsters Are Responsible for Church Burnings / 137

FOCUS: *Suggestions for Further Reading* / 139
DEVELOPING IDEAS: *About Deviance* / 141

**PART SIX** ## Social Inequality / 145

INTRODUCTION / 147

The Economic Escalator / 150

Images of Aging / 153

An Apple Pie and an Open Mind / 155

Immigrants Create Jobs for Americans (with William J. Leong) / 158

Another Crisis in Black and White? / 161

FOCUS: *Suggestions for Further Reading* / 163

DEVELOPING IDEAS: *About Social Inequality* / 166

**PART SEVEN** ## Social Change / 169

INTRODUCTION / 171

The Boomerang Effect in Planning Social Change / 175

Fads / 178

Riding the Rumor Mill / 181

Highway to Hell? / 185

Enquiring Times / 188

FOCUS: *Suggestions for Further Reading* / 191

DEVELOPING IDEAS: *About Social Change* / 193

**INTO THE FUTURE** / 195

**BIBLIOGRAPHY / 203**

**INDEX / 209**

# ■ ABOUT THE AUTHOR

**Jack Levin** is the Irving and Betty Brudnick Professor of Sociology and Criminology at Northeastern University. He has authored and coauthored a number of books, including *Elementary Statistics in Social Research*, *The Functions of Discrimination and Prejudice*, *Gossip: The Inside Scoop*, *Hate Crimes: The Rising Tide of Bigotry and Bloodshed*, and *Overkill: Mass Murder and Serial Killing Exposed*. His work has appeared in professional journals, including *Youth & Society*, *Criminology*, *The Gerontologist*, and *Sex Roles*, as well as in the *New York Times*, the *Boston Globe*, the *Detroit Free Press*, and the *Chicago Tribune*. He has lectured on campuses across the country. A dedicated educator and social advocate, Jack Levin received Northeastern University's Excellence in Teaching Award and was honored by the Council for Advancement and Support of Education as its Professor of the Year in Massachusetts.

# ■ ABOUT THE PUBLISHER

Pine Forge Press is a new educational publisher, dedicated to publishing innovative books and software throughout the social sciences. On this and any other of our publications, we welcome your comments and suggestions.

Please call or write us at:

>PINE FORGE PRESS
>A Sage Publications Company
>2455 Teller Road
>Thousand Oaks, CA 91320
>(805) 499-4224
>E-mail: sales@pfp.sagepub.com

Visit our new World Wide Web site, your direct link to a multitude of online resources: www.sagepub.com/pineforge

# Preface

Sociology is a vitally exciting field. You may know that and I may know that. The trick is getting our students to realize it. Usually, instructors who teach introductory sociology hope that they will develop in their students some enthusiasm for the contributions of the field, but the question is always *how*.

I wrote this book with at least two specific outcomes in mind, both of which relate to the general goal of getting the students to understand and appreciate the sociological perspective:

1. To serve as a springboard to more abstract thinking about society
2. To encourage student interest in learning more about the field of sociology

It is an important function of sociology to help broaden the educational experience of all college students, but especially those in fields of study that may be narrow in scope and purpose. One measure of the effectiveness of an introductory sociology course is the extent to which students come to view their world with a sociological eye.

When students truly "see" the sociology in things, they are also being helped to develop their abstract thinking skills—the very skills that are of vital importance in any job or career. Unfortunately, students too often get little help from their introductory courses in enhancing their ability to think at an abstract level. Instead, they are asked to read and memorize long lists of terms that seem more to obfuscate and complicate than to clarify reality.

The snapshots in this book are casual and informal, but they are designed to ease students into the formal world of sociological analysis. Each essay relates some abstract sociological concepts to the concrete problems confronting ordinary people. Social structure and social change are introduced as major variables but almost always in the context of everyday life.

At the same time, the snapshots are grounded in sociological data and theorizing. The introductory essays that lead each section are intended to emphasize the importance of the formal sociological literature. Indeed, the entire book serves as a springboard from the informal, concrete world of the student to the more formal, abstract world of sociological theory and method.

Students also need active ways for developing their ability to see and articulate abstractions and for analyzing data about social reality. The physical and biological sciences usually include a "lab" component in their courses in which students are given an opportunity for hands-on experience. Sociologists should attempt, wherever possible, to do the same.

For this reason, each section of the book contains ideas for student writing and research assignments. There is nothing fancy or complicated about the proposed tasks. They are designed to get introductory students to begin to write from a sociological perspective or to collect data about their everyday lives. We can only hope that they will decide to go on to bigger and better sociological things.

To the extent that the first outcome is realized, students will, I hope, also achieve the second: They will be eager to learn more about the sociological perspective. Some will take more sociology courses or even major in the discipline.

Unlike the situation in many other fields, sociology simply cannot depend on students' prior familiarity with the study of behavior to provide a background of information or enhance their interest. In high school, very few had the opportunity to select a sociology course. Some may have a vague idea that sociologists study human behavior or that sociology is somehow related to social work, but that's about it.

Partly as a result of their lack of familiarity, only a small number of students declare a sociology major when entering college: More typically, students who enroll in introductory sociology courses represent a range of disciplines and interests. It is, therefore, a major function of the introductory sociology course—for many undergraduates, perhaps their only point of formal contact—to convince students to take upper-level courses in the field. This places a special burden on instructors to provide a positive learning climate—one in which student interest is encouraged.

Writing the third edition of *Sociological Snapshots* has given me a chance to make some important changes. Most of the snapshots found in the second edition have been retained, although several have been placed in a different section, modified, or updated. Moreover, there are nine new snapshots in this edition, some of which were written specifically for the book.

A number of people were important in making *Sociological Snapshots 3* a reality. At *Bostonia*, I am grateful to Laura Freid, who gave me the opportunity to write a regular column on behavior for a first-rate magazine; to Keith Botsford, who permitted me to carry on the tradition; and to Lori Calabro and Janice Friedman, under whose skillful editorship the quality of my writing always improved. I also thank David Gibson at *Northeastern University Magazine* for helping me to write the essay concerning the sociology of soap operas. Rachelle Cohen encouraged me to do "Americans Are Moving to the Margins of Society" for the *Boston Herald*, and Marjorie Pritchard encouraged me to write "Who's Minding the Kids?" for the *Boston Globe*.

I also depended a great deal on the insightful comments and suggestions of the following reviewers:

Paul Baker, *Illinois State University*
Agnes Riedmann, *Creighton University*
Anne Hastings, *University of North Carolina at Chapel Hill*
Robert Emerick, *San Diego State University*
Judith Richlin-Klonsy, *University of California, Los Angeles*
William R. Aho, *Rhode Island College*
Russ Crescimanno, *Piedmont Community College*
Diane Carmody, *Western Washington University*
Judith Lawler Caron, *Albertus Magnus College*
Mary Rogers, *University of West Florida*
Michael L. Sanow, *Towson State University*
Rich Eckstein, *Villanova University*
Shirley Varmette, *Southern Connecticut State*

My colleague Arnie Arluke deserves a special note of praise for suggesting the title of this book. Jamie Fox and Bill Levin were generous with both their encouragement and their ideas. Christie White was an outstanding research assistant.

Steve Rutter of Pine Forge Press made all the difference. If he made me slave over a hot PC, then it was worth every minute. No editor could have done more.

My wife, Flea, and my children, Michael, Bonnie, and Andrea, have been more than patient, tolerating all of my idiosyncrasies.

As in earlier editions, I dedicate this book to the thousands of students I have had the pleasure of teaching. They have taught me a great deal about sociology and about life.

JACK LEVIN
BOSTON, MASSACHUSETTS

Photo credits:

Visual Essays by Shelley Kowalski, University of Oregon.

Page 22-23: *Boy Scouts,* Library of Congress; *Prom Court,* Lisa Yount; *Signs of U.S. Culture,* Lisa Yount.

Page 50-51: *Little Boys,* Emily Niebrand; *Little Girls,* Emily Niebrand; *TV Zone,* Lisa Yount.

Page 78-79: *Wagon Tots,* Emily Niebrand; *Reid Reunion,* Lisa Yount; *Commencement Chaos,* Lisa Yount.

Page 98-99: *Senate Chamber,* Lisa Yount; *Prim Couple,* Shelley Kowalski; *Dancing Boys,* Shelley Kowalski.

Page 118-119: *Obese Pair,* Emily Niebrand; *Obese Student,* Emily Niebrand; *Chubby Walker,* Emily Niebrand.

Page 144-145: *Cars,* Shelley Kowalski; *Rich Man,* Shelley Kowalski; *Poor Man,* Shelley Kowalski.

Page 168-169: *Quiet Road,* Shelley Kowalski; *Highway Mess,* Shelley Kowalski.

# THE SOCIOLOGICAL EYE

Among my several hobbies, photography is my favorite. I've never tried to take formal or posed pictures. Instead, the heart of my interest—what I have always found most satisfying—is the art of taking "snapshots"—informal, often candid, photos of everyday life. I particularly enjoy capturing on film the problems experienced by ordinary people as well as the spontaneous, unguarded moments in the lives of loved ones.

The essays in this book are snapshots, too, but they are sociological snapshots. Each one is a "3 × 5 glossy" of a social situation encountered by the people we meet every day—the circumstances of ordinary people caught up in ordinary (and, occasionally, not so ordinary) social events. You will find essays about family and class reunions, television soap operas, behavior in elevators, children who have unpopular names, people who do the dirty work in occupations, bystander apathy, people who act in deviant ways while driving in automobiles, heartburn, fads through the generations, popular rumors about shopping malls, contemporary images of fat people, and so on. At the extreme end, you will also discover a few essays concerning topics such as the death penalty, mass killers, and hate crimes (sadly, in today's society, even ordinary people have to be aware of such extraordinary topics).

The essays in this book are snapshots in another sense as well: Most take a casual, informal approach with respect to the presentation of statistical evidence. Many appeared originally in *Bostonia* (a magazine of "culture and ideas"). Others were opinion pieces that I earlier published in newspapers. Some were written specifically for this book. But all of them were designed to bridge the gap existing between the "two cultures" of academic sociology and everyday life. As a result, in every snapshot, you will find a mix of both social science and journalism. There are very few references, quantitative data, and formal evidence, the kind that you typically expect to find in an introductory sociology textbook. Sometimes, the essays in the book present only anecdotal confirmation—illustrations and examples rather than hard, statistical fact. Some are speculative pieces about changes in society or about the future. Others seek to throw a new perspective on aspects of society that may have seemed obvious to you before. None is meant to replace the technical journal articles written for professional sociologists. All are meant to motivate students, to help them see the contribution of the sociological approach, and to ease them as gently as possible into the more formal world of sociological analysis.

After teaching classes in sociology for a number of years, I have noticed that many students are troubled by what they regard as the abstractness of sociological insight. They often complain about not being able to see how social structure touches their everyday lives or how culture contributes to ordinary events. No longer are they asked to examine the structure of individuals but of entire groups, organizations, institutions, communities, or societies.

What I believe is missing, from a pedagogical viewpoint, are the snapshots of culture and social structure that bridge the gap existing in many students' minds between what may appear to be vast sociological abstractions, on the one hand, and everyday experiences, on the other. Hence, the central purpose of this book: to relate abstract sociological concepts to the concrete problems confronting ordinary individuals in our society.

But please don't be fooled into believing that these snapshots represent the personal opinions of the author alone. On the contrary, all of them are based on either sociological thinking, sociological data, or both. The essays that introduce each section of the book and the annotated suggested readings at the end ("Focus: Suggestions for Further Reading") are meant to emphasize the importance of the sociological literature. Indeed, they direct the student to it. You will find that the suggested readings include not only the more formal sources on which the snapshots were based but also important general works from the sociological literature. I have tried to describe them in enough detail so that interested students will understand *why* they might be worth reading. Once again, no snapshot is meant to replace the technical journal articles—the formal portraits—written for professional sociologists, but all are grounded in them.

Nor was this book written to replace your standard introductory text. Instead, *Sociological Snapshots* was intended to serve as a springboard into the formal course material, whether presented in a single text or as a series of monographs. To move back and forth between levels of abstraction, each section of the book has been organized in a consistent format. First, there is an introductory essay in which the basic sociological concepts are defined, discussed, illustrated, and then linked with the snapshots for that particular section. Second, there are the snapshots themselves. Next, there are suggestions for further reading, extensively annotated (see the Bibliography for publication information for each reading). Finally, there are ideas for student writing and research assignments in "Developing Ideas." By the way, most of these assignments require the students to apply a sociological eye to their everyday lives or to *begin*, in a preliminary way, to collect data using a sociological method.

There is one final sense in which the essays in this book are snapshots. They often reflect, frequently in an explicit way, the ideas that the *photographer* considers to be valuable or problematic. In taking pictures of the world around me, I often take photos of my family and friends, and occasionally of the unusual circumstances of daily life, but always with a point of view implicit in my choice of subject. In other words, my snapshots are, in part, a reflection of my values—the things that I appreciate or cherish. They are often addressed to preserving and understanding the images of the people I love, the problems in everyday life that bother me, or the things I believe need changing.

Like all "scientists," sociologists have values. They are human beings too; they have grown up in a particular social setting and have been exposed selectively to certain kinds of ideas.

Max Weber, a turn-of-the-century German sociologist who contributed a great deal to our understanding of religion, inequality, and social change, strongly believed that sociology could be *value free*. He fully recognized that the subjects sociologists chose to study were frequently influenced by their personal values. For example, it would not be surprising that a sociologist who grew up in extreme poverty might decide to study inequality, a rape victim might conduct research into the causes of sexual violence, an African American sociologist might specialize in race relations, and so on.

But when Weber talked about value-free sociology, he wasn't really talking about the selection of a subject about which to conduct research. Instead, he meant that sociologists must not permit their values, their biases, or their personal opinions to interfere with their analysis of that subject. They must, instead, attempt to be objective in collecting and analyzing information; they must seek out and consider *all* of the evidence, even evidence that might contradict their personal opinions. Weber would have advised that we must let the chips fall where they may. I hope my personal biases have determined only the subjects of my snapshots, not the conclusions that I reach about them.

Now that you understand the *snapshot* part of the title of this book, *Sociological Snapshots 3*, I ask that you stop a moment longer and consider the *sociological* part as well. As you probably already surmise—even if you have never taken a course in psychology—it deals with the behavior and personality of *individual* human beings. Psychologists might study a person's attitudes, hostility, attractiveness, moods, helpfulness, learning style, prejudices, and so on. In contrast, sociologists focus not on any one individual but on what happens *between* two or more individuals when they interact. Sociologists might study the relationship between husband and wife, interaction in a small task group at work, the peer groups in a high school, family relations, prison culture, relations between managers and workers, and so on.

To explain the unique and important contribution of sociology, allow me to reveal a little bit about my everyday routine. Every time I drive from my suburban home to my office in the city, I think about how painfully predictable and orderly my daily commuting routine has become. I live some 25 miles from downtown, so I have plenty of time, while sitting in bumper-to-bumper traffic, to think. In my darker, more impatient moments, I play "what if" games: What if I had sold my house and moved into the city? What if I were teaching in a college located in a remote, rural area? What if I had taken the train into work? What if I could change my schedule to avoid the rush hour commute? *Would I still be stuck in traffic? Probably not.*

As a sociologist, I am particularly interested in the fact that my predicament is shared by so many other people. This, of course, explains why traffic jams happen on a daily basis. Tens of thousands of residents have similar work schedules, live in the suburbs, and drive their cars to work in the city. They get up at about the same time every morning, take a shower, brush their teeth, and have a cup of coffee. Then, they take to the roads—most of them at the same time that I do!

Sociologists seek to understand the predictable and *patterned* aspects of what happens between people when they get together; sociologists even have a term for it: *social structure*. And in the case of sitting in maddening bumper-to-bumper traffic every day, social structure has become my biggest headache.

The smallest unit of social structure informs us that every member of society is expected to behave in a certain way, depending on the social position he or she occupies at any given time. Known as a *role*, this bundle of expected behaviors varies, from stopping at red lights and yielding the right-of-way at intersections if you are a driver or giving lectures and grading exams if you are a teacher, to conversing informally and being supportive if you are a friend. In the role of physician, an individual is expected to give physical exams and treat illnesses, whereas in the role of homemaker, an individual is expected to feed children and provide shelter. Dentists can stick their fingers in your mouth, but only during working hours. Shoe salesmen can measure your foot size, unless they happen to be in church. And judges can order you in contempt of court, except when they are eating in a restaurant or mowing the lawn at home. In truth, everybody plays a number of different roles every day. The same person who is a dentist may also be a parent, someone's child, a member of the PTA at school, a part-time student at night, a member of a religious congregation, a vice president of a professional organization, a patient, a customer in stores and restaurants, a good friend, a brother or sister, a spouse, and so on. Each and every role played has its own set of expected behaviors and, typically, we play large numbers of roles every day.

In "Just How Powerful Is a Role?" we learn that many people will go to great lengths, acting in uncharacteristic and bizarre ways, simply to behave in the socially expected manner. The experiment described in this essay suggests that roles can be very powerful in terms of determining how we behave and may also help us understand how the most hideous atrocities are sometimes committed by normal, even healthy and stable, individuals.

The negative consequences of social structure can be seen in other ways as well. In "Better Late Than Never," we see that college students are usually expected to "bloom" on time. That is, they are supposed to excel academically from an early age and to enter college by the age of 18 or 19. Indeed, if they vary from the expected pattern, students are given a name. They are called "late bloomers."

Of course, whether or not a student is ultimately successful in the classroom (and in a career) is partially a matter of individual effort, talent, and luck. But there is definitely an important sociological side to being successful as well. *You probably won't excel academically if you are denied the opportunity to do so.*

Traditionally, men were much more likely than women, no matter how qualified in terms of grades and test scores, to be given any opportunity for higher education. Similarly, it was far more probable for individuals who were born into wealthy circumstances to attend college than for their economically less fortunate counterparts.

Opportunity also varies by society. In most societies, blooming on time is strictly enforced, no matter how much potential an individual might have. You either go to college at the age of 18 or not at all; you either get As and Bs by the time you're 12 years old or you receive a trade school education, at best. In American society, we still prefer blooming on schedule—the majority of college students fit the mold—but we also allow some flexibility as to timing. In fact, 25% of all college students are now over 30, and close to 20% of college freshmen had Cs and Ds in high school.

Of course, social structure also has its desirable aspects. Because social life is somewhat predictable, we are able to count on instructors meeting their classes, count on doctors making their appointments, count on final exams to begin and end pretty much on time, and so on. Because of the strict scheduling of time in an educational context, school administrators definitely benefit, because they can predict with some degree of certainty precisely how many textbooks, classrooms, and teachers they will need for an upcoming academic year. In fact, it would not be too much of an exaggeration to suggest that life without some degree of social order—social structure—would be utterly chaotic and therefore impossible over the long run. Perhaps the rush-hour commute is unpleasant, but at least we can be fairly sure that classes will be held when scheduled and that shops, stores, and restaurants will be open when they are expected to be.

In "Heartburn and Modern Times," I suggest that even basic biological processes (the regurgitation of stomach acid back into the esophagus, causing the burning sensation we call *heartburn*) may be influenced by a weakening of social structure. French sociologist Émile Durkheim, who lived at the turn of the century, used the term *anomie* to describe a social situation in which the traditional rules of everyday life have broken down and individuals become confused as to how to behave. Because of a sudden and dramatic change in lifestyle, their old patterns of social interaction are disturbed and new patterns have not yet been established. Individuals caught in an anomic condition are therefore at a loss to know how they are expected to behave. Social life is, for them, no longer patterned, shared, or predictable.

A state of anomie can be brought on by any of several different circumstances—for example, war, a physical disaster, a dramatic drop in income, or the loss of family and friends. Communities that attract large numbers of transients, drifters, and migrants often experience anomic conditions. For example, many who move great distances from home for the sake of a job have left behind all sources of guidance and support—their friends, extended kin, church, and fraternal organizations. After arriving in Los Angeles or Miami or Houston, they may have no place to turn for counsel or advice.

In his classic work *Suicide: A Study in Sociology* (1951), Durkheim discovered that anomie actually provoked some individuals to commit suicide. More precisely, he found that the rate of suicide in an area increases during periods of rapid social or economic change and also among those who are recently divorced or widowed. If anomie affects the rate of suicide, it should be less than shocking to discover that anomie produces high rates of antacid use as well. Indeed, anomic circumstances seem to be associated with all forms of pathology, including crime, suicide, and even heartburn. Notice, by the way, that I address the *rate* of pathology, including antacid use, rather than any individual who experiences heartburn. I am not suggesting that the newcomers in any metropolitan area necessarily suffer with heartburn (though this is possible), only that their presence in large numbers will increase the likelihood that the heartburn rate is generally high. Maybe it's the transients and drifters who have heartburn, or perhaps they give it to more stable members of the population. As a sociologist, I am characterizing the metropolitan area as a whole, even if I never look at an individual case. In sum: The state of some characteristic of the area (its degree of migration) may have some influence on its rate of acid indigestion, not to mention its rate of suicide, homicide, and divorce. ∎

# Just How Powerful Is a Role?
## Ask the Prisoners and Guards on Campus

Is it possible for people who are ordinarily decent, caring, and kind to behave as though they are sadistic and cruel, just because we expect them to be? Can the structure of social situations make normal people do crazy, sickening, immoral things?

At the Nuremberg trials for crimes against humanity perpetrated in the concentration camps during World War II, Nazi leaders typically looked so normal, so ordinary, so much like the rest of us. Yet they were eventually found guilty of organizing and carrying out mass executions. In addition, thousands of German citizens went along and obeyed orders, even if it meant committing atrocities.

An important study by Philip Zimbardo and his associates at Stanford University may help shed light on the phenomenon of normal people doing abnormal, even horrific, things to others. Zimbardo and his colleagues turned the basement of a building on campus into a mock prison. They created a number of cells by installing bars and locks on each room and then placing a cot in each one.

Twenty student volunteers—all chosen for their mature and stable personalities—were selected to participate in the study. On a purely random basis (i.e., the flip of a coin), half of the students were assigned to play the role of guards, and the other half were assigned to play the role of prisoners.

The experiment actually started at the homes of the 10 student prisoners. To increase the realism of the study, all of them were arrested, put in handcuffs, read their rights, and then driven to jail in police cars. They were then completely stripped, sprayed with disinfectants, issued prison uniforms, and placed into locked cells.

Everyone knew that the experiment was artificial and that it was supposed to end in 2 weeks. Nobody was really a prisoner; nobody was really a guard. It was pure make-believe; it had been decided by the flip of a coin. Yet after only a few days, both the prisoners and the guards were playing their roles with frightening determination.

Guards were told only to keep order. Instead, they began to humiliate and embarrass the prisoners, coercing them to remain silent on command, to sing or laugh in front of the other inmates, and to clean up messes made by the guards. In some cases, the guards would verbally and physically threaten and intimidate the prisoners, apparently for the purpose of asserting their authority.

For their part, the prisoners became more and more passive and compliant. In accordance with the roles to which they had been assigned, the prisoners obeyed orders and accepted commands, no matter how unreasonable. They began to feel totally powerless to fight back. After only 6 days, four of the prisoners had to be excused from the study, as they had suffered serious episodes of anxiety, anger, or depression. In fact, the entire experiment was ended in less than 1 week when it became clear that the guards had become abusive and the prisoners were emotionally at risk.

Interviews conducted after the experiment ended were revealing. Both the prisoners and the guards told Zimbardo and his associates that they were both shocked and ashamed at how they had behaved. None of them would have predicted that they were capable of such cruelty, in the case of the guards, or obedience to authority, in the case of the prisoners. Remember that all of the student volunteers had been selected for their mature and stable personalities. Yet they all acted according to the roles created by the structure of prison life.

How powerful is a role? Just ask the students who volunteered to participate in Zimbardo's study. Then think of the atrocities committed in Nazi Germany! ■

# Better Late Than Never
Individual Success Doesn't Always Follow a Strict Schedule

Dr. William Levin is a professor of sociology at Bridgewater State College, an award-winning teacher, and a prolific and respected author in his field. He also flunked the eighth grade.

I met Bill Levin almost 20 years ago as his master's thesis adviser in what was then the School of Public Communication at Boston University. We hit it off almost immediately. Not only did we share the same last name (though not the same parents), we also discovered we were both educational late bloomers—mediocre high school students who later developed into serious-minded, dedicated college students (I can't say that I flunked the eighth grade, but I can still "brag" about being on academic probation during my first year as an undergraduate at American International College).

Bill Levin's escape from educational mediocrity is far from unique. In fact, there are thousands of educational late bloomers who go on to become brilliant college or graduate students. Thousands more interrupt their collegiate pursuits, only to return years later. In fact, we live in a society in which second chances are fast becoming a way of life, especially in the educational field.

We tolerate late blooming, but do we know why? Trying to answer just that question, Bill and I recently talked with a number of college students. And in interviews with both late and early bloomers, we were able to identify four important factors: capacity, opportunity, some triggering event, and a period of readiness to accept change in which social support is present.

Intellectual capacity is a prerequisite for almost any success, whenever it occurs in the life cycle. But for late bloomers, capacity has an important emotional component. Those who lack intellectual capacity more than make up for it with commitment and involvement. Many of the late bloomers we interviewed were, as high school students, almost fanatically devoted to a cause, a hobby, a job, a sport, or an idea. For example, while in high school, one late bloomer became committed to physical exercise. Hard-pressed to find the time to study, he still managed to jog, run, lift weights, bike, and swim on a regular basis. Another student was heavily into illicit drugs. He spent hours in the library, but not doing his homework. Instead, he read and researched articles related to his addiction. Then there was the mechanical engineering major who now has a 3.6 grade point average but had only a 2.5 average in high school. He, however, was a member of his school's debating team and chorus in addition to working more than 20 hours a week.

In a sense, the presence of emotional commitment in high school may indicate later academic potential. The question is, how do we transfer that commitment from an extracurricular activity, athletics, or a cause to the college classroom?

Part of the answer involves the second factor in late blooming: the presence of opportunity. Almost everywhere outside the United States, the timing of academic success is inflexible. Students must achieve high grades and appropriate scores on standardized tests early in their academic careers; they must also enter college by a specified age. In England, India, and Japan, for example, students who have not excelled by the time they reach high school are effectively disqualified as college material. What is more, students are expected to enroll in college by their late teens and are not given opportunities to do so later in life, regardless of their potential. Even after the educational reforms of the post-World War II era, highly structured lines of study separating high school attendance from access to college remain the modal pattern around the rest of the world.

In sharp contrast, the American educational system gives students a second, third, even a fourth chance for a college education. If they or their parents are able to pay the bills, even students who have low grades in high school are granted an opportunity to enroll in higher education. One third of all colleges have open admission policies. Moreover, hundreds of thousands of students who begin at community and junior colleges later transfer into 4-year institutions. The increasing number of women who return to college after raising children provides a significant new pool of potential late bloomers. Similarly, the increasing acceptance of midlife career changes has created an entirely new category of late, late bloomers who continue their education after spending decades in the workforce.

But capacity and opportunity are not always enough for late blooming to occur. Bill Levin, for example, had the opportunity to attend college because his parents saved the money to send him. And like millions of other middle-class students, he went to college primarily because that's what was expected of him. But for Levin and others like him, the commitment to education only materialized because of a triggering event—a reward, a punishment, or both that provided a rationale for making a profound change in their lifestyle.

For some of the late bloomers we studied, that triggering event was a work experience during college. Some suggested that a job showed them, perhaps for the first time, the strong connection between grades and the kind of work they were likely to do after they graduated. Even an unpleasant job during college was motivating; it forced them to deal with the likelihood that unless things changed drastically, this was the kind of boring, monotonous work they might expect to be doing for the rest of their lives.

Other late bloomers pointed to more positive events as triggering their commitment to academics. Some, such as Bill Levin, gave credit to a great teacher who had inspired them to study or to a course that was new and exciting to them. Others were a few years older than their classmates: They had dropped out to work for a year or two, transferred from another college, or spent a few years in the military. Peers also made a difference. For example, one late-blooming college senior reported that it was a bright, achievement-oriented girlfriend who motivated him by threatening to end their relationship if he didn't "buckle down."

If the series of triggering events is effective, a student enters a period of readiness to change when social support and encouragement become extremely important. During this stage, the academic community gradually becomes an important reference point, a source of norms and values as well as a source of guidance. The student frequently changes his or her major based on personal interest rather than practicality or parental guidance. For the first time, grades are used as markers of personal worth and school takes on primary importance.

The individual is ready to bloom. He talks informally with instructors during their office hours and after classes; she discusses a lecture with her friends. He spends more time in the library; she writes for the campus newspaper and runs for student government. In this stage, instructors, advisers, and friends can make a huge difference. The student is ready to bloom, but he or she still looks for and needs the help of others on campus.

At the time I first met Bill Levin, he had recently discovered the social sciences. Within a year, he had become totally immersed in graduate student culture. Like so many of his early-blooming classmates, he read, talked, and slept sociology; it became the focal point of his life.

It is legitimate to ask whether it is worth focusing so much attention on late bloomers. After all, aren't they less successful than their counterparts who achieve "on time"? Actually, one of the few studies to compare late and early bloomers concludes just the opposite. Scientists whose educational achievements came relatively late were more productive than those scientists who achieved early. Educational burnout may be less severe for late bloomers, not only because they begin later to achieve in earnest but also because they are more likely to achieve for their own sake rather than for the sake of a parent. The success of a late bloomer may be particularly sweet. You've heard the expression "Better late than never." Have you ever considered the possibility "Better late than early," at least where education is concerned?

Given our present state of knowledge, we are not able to predict who will and will not turn out to be a late bloomer. Until our theories and methods permit such accurate predictions, we must treat every student as a potential late bloomer. This means that we must never give up on anyone. Bill Levin is living proof, and he has plenty of company. ∎

# Heartburn and Modern Times
Don't Blame the Tex-Mex

According to a Gallup survey conducted several years ago, the ailment known as heartburn is a chronic source of pain and suffering for almost 62 million American adults. Fifty-four percent of them pin the blame on spicy foods; others single out overeating, indigestion, gas, or poor diet. Many regularly take an antacid in pill or liquid form.

For the sufferer, heartburn clearly has a biological basis. It frequently occurs after a meal when acid backs up from the stomach into the esophagus, causing a burning sensation in the chest or throat. From a sociological point of view, however, there may be a good deal more to heartburn than just the discomfort of spicy foods and excessive acidity. Like many other physical ailments, the symptoms of heartburn may be influenced by the stresses and strains frequently associated with residential mobility undertaken to enhance a career or supposedly improve the quality of life.

I ranked 197 metropolitan areas of the United States on the *National Rolaids Heartburn Index*, a measure based on an area's per-capita sales of all brands of over-the-counter antacids, and then compared these metropolitan areas on a grid of important social, economic, and demographic characteristics. Most striking, I found important regional differences in heartburn rates. For example, despite their reputation for having a laid-back pace of life, most major cities located in the far West—San Francisco, Sacramento, Fresno, Seattle, Los Angeles, and Phoenix—had particularly high rates of antacid use. Indeed, 40% of all high-heartburn metropolitan areas were located in western states. Also having particularly high rates were southern cities such as Charlotte, North Carolina; Richmond, Virginia; and New Orleans, Louisiana.

By contrast, centrally located cities had extremely low rates of heartburn. Green Bay, Wisconsin; Sioux City, Iowa; Columbia, Missouri; and Fort Smith, Arkansas placed close to the bottom. In fact, almost half of the 40 metropolitan areas with the lowest rates of heartburn were located in midwestern and southern states. But the lowest of them all was located in El Paso, Texas, which, with its penchant for spicy Tex-Mex cuisine, turned out to have the lowest level of heartburn of any city in the United States.

Data on northeastern cities were also surprising. Overall, those cities seldom exhibited either high or low heartburn levels. Only 11% of both the highest heartburn metropolitan areas and the lowest heartburn areas were located in the Northeast. New York City, for example, registered only a moderate rate of heartburn, though it is well-known for its fast-paced, hectic way of life.

How can these variations in rates of antacid use by metropolitan area be explained? Differences in diet and physical environment might contribute to the overall level of heartburn. Over-the-counter antacid use may not be an accurate measure of heartburn (a few people without heartburn take these antacids and many with heartburn do not).

Despite such methodological problems, a major contributing factor to the rate of heartburn in an area can be found in what might be called "gold rush fever." All of the cities with a high incidence of heartburn have recently experienced tremendous population growth as a result of migration from other cities and regions of the country. For the sake of a job or a better way of life, former midwesterners and easterners have "gone west." They have packed their bags, left behind family and friends, and traveled thousands of miles to cities on the West Coast. This may explain why most of the most attractive and appealing metropolitan areas also have the highest rates of heartburn. They attract individuals who are dissatisfied with their present lives and are willing to move to enhance them.

Cities with stable populations are more likely to have a low incidence of heartburn. These cities appeal less to individuals who want to increase their economic opportunities. In such cities, construction comes to a standstill as the demand for real estate remains constant. Of the top 15 housing markets, not one is located in a low-heartburn metropolitan area, but 5 are in the high-heartburn group. The city of El Paso never experienced the oil-based, boom-and-bust cycle of heartburn-plagued Texas cities such as Dallas and Houston.

Wherever there are large numbers of transient, rootless people, there is also likely to be anxiety, stress, frustration . . . and high levels of heartburn. Sociologists call this state of affairs *anomie*, a social condition that prevails where newcomers to an area are confused as to the rules of living. When things are anomic, there is widespread disorganization and isolation, a breakdown in order.

One indicator of anomie is the presence of social pathology. Thus, high-heartburn areas were more likely than their low-heartburn counterparts to also have high rates of violent crime, divorce, and alcohol consumption. Heartburn may be another, albeit more subtle, indicator that something is wrong.

Other researchers have noticed that the pathology varies by specific metropolitan areas. Social psychologist Robert Levine of California State University compared cities in terms of their level of psychological stress. He found that the 6 of his 10 cities with the highest stress were located in the far West. He determined that stress was especially high in those metropolitan areas that contained large numbers of migrants, residents who were born out of state. Not coincidentally, the western states had the greatest percentage of migrants—gold rush fever strikes again!

Census Bureau data suggest that the population flow to the far West may be on the verge of reversing itself. In the future, easterners and midwesterners may cease exporting their heartburn to other areas of the country. Who knows? New York, Philadelphia, or Boston might even become the next heartburn capital of the United States. ■

---

■ **FOCUS** *Suggestions for Further Reading*

The classic prison role experiment conducted by Philip Zimbardo and his colleagues Craig Haney and William Banks is described in detail in "A Pirandellian Prison" in *The New York Times Magazine* (1973). For a famous study of obedient role-playing, also read Stanley Milgram's *Obedience to Authority: An Experimental View* (1974). In Milgram's study, 60% of a sample of normal Americans was willing to administer a severe electrical shock to a stranger simply because they were told to do so by an authority figure in a lab coat. The concept of role continues to be represented as an important part of the sociological literature. Helen Rose Fuchs Ebaugh (1988), for example, has studied the process of shedding a role—of becoming an ex-member—and therefore of eliminating strong social identities. More recently, Rosalind Barnett (1994) has examined the relationships among the diverse roles that an individual sometimes plays. In an article, "Home-to-Work Spillover Revisited," Barnett looks at how the marital and parental roles of women in dual-career families can minimize the bad experiences on the job.

Concerning "Better Late Than Never," Bill Levin and I published our ideas about late blooming in an article titled "Sociology of Educational Late-Blooming" in *Sociological Forum* (1991). More recently, I wrote more about the triggering incidents for late blooming in "Misery as a Turning Point for Academic Success" in the *Journal of Research in Education* (1993).

Eviatar Zurubavel's book *Hidden Rhythms: Schedules and Calendars in Social Life* (1981) offers insights into a much neglected topic, the sociology of time. For a social-historical analysis of the rise of age consciousness in American society, read Howard Chudacoff's *How Old Are You?* (1989). In this fascinating work, he reminds us that there was a time when people didn't know their precise ages and when birthdays were left uncelebrated. Prior to the 20th century, people rarely sent birthday cards to one another or had birthday parties.

The data reported in "Heartburn and Modern Times" concerning rates of antacid use by metropolitan area were originally collected by pollster A. C. Nielson. I was hired by Warner Lambert to analyze these data and then report my results to them.

The link between heartburn and anomie is a new variation on an old theme. Anomic circumstances have long been associated with high rates of pathology. In his classic study *Suicide: A Study in Sociology* (1951), Émile Durkheim introduces a sociological theory to explain differences in the rate of suicide by time and place. One of his major types is called anomic suicide because it results from a sharp break, a profound disruption in the social bond.

By the way, Robert Levine (1997) has more recently studied the pace of life in cities around the United States and in 31 countries around the world. Apparently, pace of life creates a series of stresses that are not dependent on attracting large numbers of migrants to a metropolitan area. In fact, relatively stable Boston—hardly a headquarter of heartburn—was determined to have the fastest pace of life among major cities in the United States.

The powerful attraction of social structure is poignantly illustrated in Debra Renee Kaufman's excellent account of *Rachel's Daughters* (1991). Her subjects were women who returned to religious orthodoxy out of a sense that structure was missing from their lives. By contrast, the extraordinary women in Mary Catherine Bateson's *Composing a Life* (1990) chose a different course in response to ambiguities in the female role. Making the best of the severe discontinuities in their lives, they improvised opportunities for creativity and innovation, but not without experiencing pain. ■

## ■ DEVELOPING IDEAS  *About Social Structure*

1. Research topic: One of the most fundamental forms of social order is contained in the concept of *role,* the set of expected behaviors associated with a particular social position such as teacher, doctor, son, mother, student, and so on. What is OK in one role may be totally inappropriate in another. For example, we expect students to take exams, write papers, and attend class. We do not expect them to stick their fingers in someone's mouth. But dentists do it every day (we actually pay dentists to stick their fingers in our mouths), and we don't expect dentists to write papers. What is proper or improper depends on the role. As you know, there is even a role of elevator rider. Similarly, there is a role of passenger, whether on a bus, train, or airplane. While riding with strangers on public transportation, we are expected to behave in a certain way. To examine the requirements of this role, take a ride on a bus or other form of public transportation (if this is too difficult, try riding in an elevator). While acting as a passenger, notice how other riders are sitting or standing, whether there is any conversation (if so, about what and under what circumstances?), and how you feel when the vehicle is crowded and why you feel that way. If you are not too embarrassed to do so, you might try starting a conversation with another passenger. What is the reaction?

2. Writing topic: In the essay about educational late bloomers, I presented several factors that seem to contribute to succeeding behind schedule, including intellectual capacity, opportunity, a precipitating incident, and social support. Think of someone you know (perhaps a friend or a relative) who possessed the intelligence to bloom educationally but never did. In a short essay, explain how his or her position in the social structure (gender identity, age, socioeconomic status, societal membership) may have helped prevent his or her educational success.

3. Writing topic: In the essay about heartburn, I focused on per-capita antacid use by metropolitan area. How do you think a psychologist who was interested in the causes of heartburn would have conducted this study? Would he or she have exam-

ined a number of metropolitan areas? What do you think he or she would have looked for in those individuals who suffered from heartburn? What conclusions might a psychologist have drawn and how might they have differed from those derived by a sociologist?

4. Research topic: One measure of the importance of being on time is just how precisely individuals keep their clocks and watches running. Because the importance of precise time varies from society to society, it is possible that the precision of watches and clocks also varies from place to place. Because it is unreasonable to ask you to travel to another society, instead compare the clocks and watches in your own home, apartment, or dormitory floor with those in someone else's home, apartment, or dormitory floor. (You might, for example, compare men's and women's floors to determine the influence of gender on the importance of time, or you might compare different kinds of office buildings.) Write down the error (from actual time as determined from the phone company, a radio or TV program, or some other objective source) on each clock or watch and then take an average for each place. Also include the number of watches and clocks in a state of disrepair. Now, identify the winning group!

5. Writing topic: Instant millionaires—those who win the Megabucks lottery—aren't always as happy as you might believe. Many of them experience tremendous anomie. In a short essay, speculate as to exactly how the lives of instant millionaires might abruptly change for the worse. Also indicate what you think they might do to minimize the pain of suddenly being wealthy.

6. Research topic: Interview someone who has recently experienced a dramatic change in lifestyle—an individual who has moved thousands of miles, has been recently widowed or divorced, or has even married. (It would be great, but very difficult, to interview an instant millionaire!) Try to determine whether the abrupt change in that person's way of life has had any negative effects of which he or she is aware. Where does he or she go for help and guidance? Is he or she more anxious about the future? How does that person fill the hours of the day with meaningful activities? If he or she has had little or no trouble adjusting, you might want to determine why. Through friendships, religion, fraternal organizations, or a commitment to work, has that person found a new source of structure in his or her life? ■

# PART ONE

## Culture

Culture can be defined as the unique shared traits, beliefs, and practices of a group. When we think of culture, we may think of the exotic, hopelessly foreign language and rituals of African tribes or South Sea Islanders. Rarely do we think of the *American Way of Life* as a culture. But, as these snapshots and essays show, from our most private moments to our most public events, the culture of the good old U.S. of A. is complex and unique.

Several of the students in the course I teach on the sociology of violence came from other countries to attend school in Boston. Two were from Asia, one was from Europe, one was from South America, and one was from an island in the Caribbean. About 15 minutes into our first meeting, I realized that their presence in the classroom would make a difference in the way I approached the course. It really didn't take a psychic to figure out that communication would be more difficult. From the first day, there were lots of bewildered looks and blank stares to remind me. Then there were questions.

At first, I considered the problem to be only one of language. In plain English, I believed that my plain English was, to them, not so plain. By the end of our first session together, however, I recognized that the problem was more profound than just misunderstood words and phrases. Indeed, from the types of questions they were asking, I concluded that some of the international students in my class also lacked familiarity with those practices, objects, and ideas that most Americans share on an everyday basis and therefore take for granted as the "American way of life." My foreign students were, in a word, unfamiliar with American *culture*. Consider a concrete example. In our discussion of the manner in which mass killings are reported by the mass media, I introduced James Huberty's rampage through a McDonald's fast-food restaurant located in a suburb of San Diego. I noted that several newspapers around the country had referred to Huberty's killing spree (he killed 21, mostly Hispanic children) as "Mass McMurder" and "The Big Mac Attack." The American students immediately understood the glib, possibly offensive aspects of these newspaper headlines, but three of the international students had only questions: "What is a Big Mac?" one asked. Not knowing the logo of this famous hamburger chain, another wanted to know why the paper called Huberty's attack "McMurder." Before continuing our discussion of mass killings, therefore, we spent several minutes talking about fast-food hamburgers.

Now, it is true that degree of familiarity with American culture varies quite a bit among the peoples of the world. And among my international students, I noticed immense variation in this respect. In fact, the young woman from Western Europe was quite familiar with American values and customs, at least much more so than her counterparts from Asia or South America. Though she had been in the United States only a few days before the course began, she had eaten many times in American fast-food restaurants (McDonald's are located throughout Europe), had watched American television, and was also acquainted more with the American brand of humor. That was because the values and customs in her own country were so similar to ours. They were likely to be, of course, because we Americans have had enormous contact with Europe and have derived much of our culture from it. The process whereby cultural traits spread from one society to another (e.g., from the "Mother Country" England to the United States) is known as *cultural diffusion*.

Clearly, we can thank (or blame) cultural diffusion for giving us many important ideas and objects that originated in, or at least passed first through, Europe. In "The Immaculate Americans," we discover that it was the British who, during the Industrial Revolution, were plumbing pioneers. By the early part of the 20th century, however, the idea of plumbing for the masses had crossed the Atlantic Ocean, and American society had taken the lead in developing private bathrooms for the majority of its citizens. For the first time in history, the home bathroom was regarded as a middle-class necessity. Also in "The Immaculate Americans," we learn that collective tolerance for odor varies from place to place, from one society to another. In some other parts of the world, Americans are viewed as neurotically concerned with their personal cleanliness. We certainly do use tremendous amounts of deodorant and mouthwash; such products have become part of our culture.

The ideas that we often take for granted or believe to be constants in nature—for example, our ideas about cleanliness—may actually originate in the culture that we learn. But what is the origin of culture? We know that people aren't born with it—although they are born with the *capacity* for culture. Only humans seem to have the full-blown capability; other animals often share a way of life but not one that is learned and passed along to the next generation. For the most part, animals are programmed from birth to act and react in social situations. (For example, birds don't learn to fly by watching other birds do it first, nor do mother birds teach them. They develop the ability for flight by instinct alone.)

The origin of a particular type of cultural content—whether one or another thing is regarded as proper and right—is also a fascinating question. Some sociologists and anthropologists believe that economics may play a major role in determining the particular character of a culture. The important 19th-century theorist Karl Marx argued, in writing about the rise of communism, that the economic system of a society determines almost everything about other social institutions. He believed that religion, family life, and the press were all "handmaidens" to the prevailing economic system; that is, they existed essentially to support and maintain the economic status quo, to make sure that it survived. From a Marxian point of view, therefore, the Protestant belief about work—the religious conviction that hard work is a sign of personal salvation—exists only because capitalism needs a way to dupe or mislead workers; that is, a way of motivating workers to tolerate their terrible working conditions, accept their exploitation by the owners of production, and be achievement oriented in the interest of maximizing corporate profit.

You don't have to accept Marxism to agree that he was right to emphasize the role of the economy in determining the complexion of "mass" culture—popular art and music—in a capitalistic society like ours. Middle-aged rock musicians such as Van Morrison, Paul Simon, Mick Jagger, and Billy Joel may not help to preserve capitalism, but their continuing popularity is probably a result of the appeal they have to huge numbers of people who grew up in the 1960s and 1970s and who are willing to spend their hard-earned money in the interest of nostalgia.

In "Baby Boomers: A Generation Without a Gap," we are introduced to a possibly important source of cultural expression. The baby boomers—that generation of people born between 1946 and 1964—continue to have plenty of cultural clout but only so long as they spend their money. How will they be treated if they give up their credit cards? Only time will tell.

Culture often takes on human form and substance. The cultural values cherished by Americans are embodied in the heroes we choose to revere on a collective level. During the opening decades of the 20th century, our cultural heroes were what sociologist Leo Lowenthal in 1961 called "idols of production"—industrial tycoons who served as role models for citizens who accepted some version of the American Dream and aspired to be successful and wealthy . . . *just like their heroes.* By midcentury, however, Americans had shifted from idols of production to idols of consumption—the entertainers and sports figures who filled our leisure hours with their music, drama, and athletic prowess.

In "The Demise of Bystander Apathy," I speculate that we have recently undergone yet another major shift in our selection of cultural heroes. Coming out of an era of spectatorship and passivity, we now seem to admire idols of activism, those men and women who are seen as having taken control of their destiny, who aren't afraid to step forward and stand apart from the crowd to take a firm position. In the face of big business and big government, we respect individuals who take charge of their everyday lives . . . because we hope to be able to do the same.

As argued in "We Are in the Midst of a Cultural Revolution," Americans' attitudes toward teenagers may be in the process of making an important, if relatively silent, cultural transformation. For 25 years or more, many children were asked to fend for themselves in the absence of structured activities and adult supervision. As increasing numbers of parents went off to work, we abandoned youth-oriented programs that might have provided healthy alternatives to violence—community centers, youth clubs, athletic activities, headstart initiatives, music programs, public skating rinks and swimming pools, and the like. Many adults simply got out of the business of raising children.

Now, for the first time in decades, we are again focusing the spotlight on our youngsters. Thanks to the growing involvement of adults—parents, teachers, neighbors, clergy, business leaders, and the police—in the lives of children, the streets of many of our major cities are safer than they have been in many years (see my "Violence Goes to School," 1998).

Culture has thus far been associated with an entire society. Yet even the smallest social settings can develop a shared set of rules for behavior—that is, a culture. In "Elevator Culture," I discuss the "proper" way to behave in an elevator when riding with other passengers. Surprisingly, perhaps, it turns out that elevator culture permits very little positive guidance for behavior—in fact, there may be only one socially correct way to stand in an elevator. No wonder some people prefer to take the stairs!

Before turning to the "snapshots" of culture in this first section of the book, let's return for a moment to the situation of having a number of international students in the small seminar that I teach. In introducing this section of the book, I emphasized the communication problems posed by my students' lack of familiarity with American culture. What I failed to stress, however, was that their presence in my seminar also had an important *positive* impact by bringing to bear on our classroom discussions the experiences of the diverse cultures they represented. In some cases, students from other countries added to our discussions by reinforcing the universal validity of our sociological generalizations. Their own experiences suggested that what was true about American society might also apply to their homelands. In other cases, however, my students added a cautionary input. Based on their experiences, certain relationships discussed in our class could probably not be generalized beyond American, or perhaps Western, culture. As a sociologist, I can safely say that I learned a great deal from being immersed, even if only on a secondhand basis, in cultures from around the world. ■

# The Immaculate Americans
Being Cleaner Doesn't Mean We're Better

Body odor is big business. Every year, we immaculate Americans spend more money on deodorants and mouthwashes than we contribute to the United Way. In addition, we probably pass more time scrubbing, washing, spraying, bathing, squirting, and gargling than any other people in the history of the world. Every American, in fact, learns from an early age that cleanliness is considered next to Godliness—a sign that an individual is morally pure and sinless. No wonder Americans spend more than 1 billion dollars annually on soap—it's part of our culture.

In other parts of the world, however, we are regarded as neurotically concerned with our personal cleanliness. In some European countries, for example, American tourists are easily identified by their demands for a room with a private bath. Meanwhile, their European counterparts more often stay in rooms where they wash up daily in a small sink and take their baths down the hall. In their own countries, anyone caught showering twice a day would probably be regarded as either eccentric or ill.

Notwithstanding our present-day preoccupation, Americans can hardly take credit (or blame) for inventing a concern for cleanliness. Arab intermediaries, in arranging a marriage, sometimes rejected a prospective bride who didn't "smell nice." Sniffing and nose kissing have long been practiced by Eskimos, Philippine Islanders, and Samoans who recognized the desire for a pleasant odor. And bathing for purification is an ancient custom practiced by the early Hebrews, Muslims, and Hindus.

Medieval royalty even took baths, but only on occasion. In England, for example, King John bathed three times a year, always before a major religious festival. But church authorities and medical practitioners in the Middle Ages generally frowned on bathing, denying the general population access to the few existing baths. Instead, medieval people stuffed their nostrils with strong perfumes to disinfect the air and reduce the onslaught of black plague. Even after the Middle Ages, Queen Elizabeth I of England bathed only monthly (whether she needed it or not).

Major efforts to overcome the problem of personal cleanliness for the masses really weren't made until the mid-19th century. During the Industrial Revolution, the British were the plumbing pioneers. For those who lacked private facilities, the state built public bathhouses consisting of individual bathrooms with centrally controlled plumbing. By the early part of the 20th century, however, cultural diffusion had taken effect, and America had taken the lead in developing private bathrooms for the majority of citizens. For the first time in history, the home bathroom was no longer viewed as a status symbol but was regarded as a middle-class necessity.

Of course, everything is relative when it comes to culture, and some Americans have acquired such lofty cultural standards today that they think foreigners smell. Perhaps they are right, at least when judged by a national norm that refuses to tolerate any body odor at all. The odorous outsiders (who, by the way, probably smell pretty much like human beings are intended to) are then regarded by some Americans as dirty, slovenly, or perhaps even morally impure.

The bias is not new. Odor has often been used to discredit entire groups of people. During the Middle Ages, for example, European Jews were widely believed to drink the blood of Christian children as part of the Passover ritual to rid themselves of an "odor of evil." It was also rumored that after their conversion to Christianity, the Jewish malodor miraculously disappeared.

Closer to home, American blacks, Latinos, Hawaiians, and Native Americans have all been stereotyped in cultural images at one time or another as smelling different. And one of the most offensive olfactory images is that of elderly citizens—especially nursing home residents—who are too often stereotyped as reeking from incontinence, indifference, and the ravages of age.

Just how accurate are such cultural images of group differences in odor? Is it possible that the members of different ethnic and racial groups really do have distinctive smells? Consider, for example, the possible effect on the quality and quantity of perspiration of dietary differences or of jobs requiring strenuous physical activity. Such differences do vary by group; they might even differ by ethnicity or social class. Yet the perception of such group differences in odor seems entirely out of proportion to their actual occurrence, if they happen at all.

More likely, the charge of minority malodor is needed by bigots who are eager to justify discriminatory treatment against a group of

*Culture*

people by dehumanizing them. The reasoning is simple enough: Animals, not human beings, give off a stench. Human beings must be treated according to the rules of civilized society, but animals can be mistreated, even slaughtered, at will. The members of group X give off a stench (they don't bathe and live like pigs), therefore they can be mistreated.

The sociological question is answered best by recognizing that perception of odor is only one component in the much larger repertoire of cultural racism. Our beliefs about various groups are often supported by deeply rooted emotions acquired early that can linger throughout life. In the Jim Crow South, white Southerners had an intense emotional reaction to the possibility of desegregating their public facilities. Black skin was regarded almost as a contagious physical condition, something dirty that might rub off and contaminate those individuals who were fortunate enough to be white—hence, the need for norms requiring separate public conveniences that imply close contact, such as restaurants, theaters, buses, water fountains, and restrooms.

In his analysis of race relations in the United States, psychiatrist James Comer, himself a black American who overcame poverty and discrimination to become a well-known psychiatrist and author, recounts the story of a white teenage girl who was scolded by her father for having put a coin in her mouth. He yelled, "Get that money out of your mouth—it might have been in a nigger's hand!" His reaction reminds us of an important principle of human behavior: You really don't have to smell like a skunk to be treated like one! ∎

# Baby Boomers
A Generation Without a Gap

Rock music has long been a symbol of adolescent rebellion. The "greasers" of the 1950s wouldn't have been caught dead listening to recordings of Glenn Miller, Woody Herman, or any other musician reminiscent of their parents' day. Similarly, members of the 1960s hip generation were too intent on distancing themselves from what they saw as oppressive traditional authority to regard tunes by Fats Domino and Chuck Berry with more than historical curiosity.

That's why it is so intriguing that today's high school and college students don't reject—and, in fact, embrace—the popular music of yesteryear. Of course, they still identify with the superstar songsters of their own age—Backstreet Boys, Hanson, Spice Girls, Fiona Apple, Oasis, and the like. But amazingly, they also admire longtime rock idols of the 1960s and early 1970s who are now well into what we euphemistically call the prime of life, otherwise known as middle age. During the past few years, oldsters such as Pink Floyd, Fleetwood Mac, Aerosmith, Carly Simon, the Grateful Dead, Mick Jagger, Van Morrison, Bonnie Raitt, George Harrison, and Paul Simon have all had top-selling CDs or videos. Simon's Grammy-winning album *Graceland* was the top-ranked compact disc just a few years ago. And according to *Billboard Magazine,* among the top concert moneymakers of the 1990s were middle-agers Billy Joel, Bob Seger, the Eagles, and David Bowie. During the same period, concerts by 1960s oldies legends like 51-year-old Gene Pitney and Shirley Alston Reeves, former lead singer of the Shirelles, drew sellout crowds. In 1997, the top concert draws continued to include an overrepresentation of middle-agers like the Rolling Stones, Paul McCartney, Barbra Streisand, and Fleetwood Mac.

Part of the continuing popularity of the 1960s rock stars is their nostalgic appeal to the moving human population explosion we now call the baby boomers, 76 million American men and women who were born between 1946 and 1964. Many of them were just coming of age during the 1960s as the Beatles, Rolling Stones, and Bob Dylan entered the music scene, or later, as Woodstock launched their generation into the 1970s. Even as their oldest members now approach their early 50s, the baby boomers wax nostalgic. They have glowing memories of the formative period in their lives and the music that it spawned.

Across the country, popular radio stations have now capitalized on this wave of nostalgia by airing programs that feature 1960s golden oldies or by sprinkling *Big Chill* hits throughout their otherwise contemporary format. But it isn't only nostalgic baby boomers who crave the sounds of the 1960s; their younger brothers and sisters and in some cases their children also do—and in a big way. It was only a few years ago, for example, that the weather vane of adolescent opinion, *Teen Magazine,* reported the results of a survey of its readers' favorite entertainers. Among the names of current idols in the entertainment world were names associated with a previous generation, many of whom are 30 years older than their teenybopper fans—Kenny Rogers, Alabama, Bill Cosby, the Judds, and Cybill Shepherd. Similarly, a poll of the youthful audience for a popular MTV all-request music program named "Heart and Soul" by the Monkees as its top video of the year and 42-year-old Davy Jones as its choice for "cutest guy." In 1998, *Seventeen* magazine raved about concerts by oldsters such as Tina Turner and focused on the future of youthful Deadheads in the aftermath of Jerry Garcia's death. Even more shocking, senior citizen singers Frank Sinatra and Tony Bennett have, during recent years, made spectacular comebacks, enjoying popularity even in the teenage music market.

Baby boomer nostalgia has also inspired many of the top advertising agencies to include pop oldies in their commercials. The fast-food company Burger King has used the Everly Brothers' "Wake Up Little Susie," the laxative Senokot employs a rendition of James Brown's "I Feel Good," and Toyota features a version of Sly and the Family Stone's "Everyday People."

Music is only one example of the baby boomers' immense and continuing cultural clout. During the 1960s, long before they were given a label, today's baby boomers had not only large numbers (half the population of the United States was under 25) but also plenty of disposable income. And they often disposed of it on 35mm single-lens reflex cameras, stereo components, bell-bottom jeans, miniskirts, Hula Hoops, and so on. Business interests were, of course, thoroughly pleased with such free-spending habits. So pleased, in fact, that commercials such as the Oil of Olay ads promised that you wouldn't look "over 25"! And in his best-selling work, *The Greening of America,* law professor Charles Reich raised the possibility that our entire society would soon be transformed in the image of youthful hippies of the day.

During the closing years of the 1960s, there was reason to make such a prediction. The baby boomers were role models for everyone who emulated their teenage children's appearance. Middle-aged women donned bell-bottom jeans, tie-dyed shirts, sandals, and love beads, while their husbands wore their hair shoulder length, their ties psychedelic, and their sideburns to the end of their ear lobes. Many also grew beards and mustaches to lengths that today would be regarded as thoroughly outrageous. Indeed, the style of the day was the style of the baby boomer generation: It seemed as if everybody was either young or wanted to be.

As we make the transition to a new century, the baby boomers have lost none of their cultural clout. Just as they were trendsetters as youths, so they are now setting trends as middle-aged adults. The baby boomers still boast large numbers and still spend lots of money. Of course, their consumer habits have changed with age and the times: They now buy VCRs, microwave ovens, compact disc players, home theaters, and personal computers. But the fact that they continue to consume is enough to explain why so many midlife models are appearing in ads and commercials.

Moreover, notwithstanding the efforts of fashion designers, few women today actually feel obligated to wear the miniskirts of a younger generation. Instead, high school and college students often follow their parents' lead by adding to their form-fitting wardrobe the loose-fitting styles formerly associated with middle age.

Will the cultural clout of baby boomers persist into old age? Will they continue to set trends in music, art, and fashion in their 60s and 70s? They will, of course, still have large numbers on their side. By the year 2025, when the baby boomers achieve senior citizenship, more than 20% of the population will be over 65. Yet it is a sad truth that numbers alone are as likely to assure poverty as power. In fact, elder Americans living 200 years ago commanded much greater respect and privilege than they do today, despite (or perhaps because of) the fact that only 10% of the population lived to celebrate their 60th birthday. Granted, this figure is skewed somewhat by high rates of infant mortality. Nonetheless, under Puritanism, old age was regarded as a sign of election and a special gift from God. But when longevity increased and more sizable numbers of people survived to old age, the cultural clout of elders declined. Specifically, preferential seating arrangements in public vehicles for older people were abolished, mandatory retirement laws appeared, youthful fashions were preferred, and eldest sons lost their inheritance advantages.

More than sheer numbers, then, graying baby boomers of the future will need to maintain the free-spending habits that endeared them to commercial interests if they are to maintain their cultural clout. Not only will they need plenty of money, but they must be willing to spend it as they did in the past. If they are anything like previous generations of older Americans, however, this may not be realistic. Senior citizens tend to become "economy conscious" by reducing their use of credit and by shopping for price. Even if many baby boomers refuse to retire at 65 or 70, they are likely to decide to temper their consumerism in favor of preparing for an uncertain future in terms of health care, economic depression, inflation, and the like. Depending on the course of public policy over the next few decades, even financially secure individuals may become quite conservative in their spending habits. This does not mean that aging baby boomers will be asked to live in poverty, only that they may be forced to give up their place as the cultural kingpins of American society. ■

# The Demise of Bystander Apathy
We Admire Idols of Activism

In 1964, in a now classic case, Kitty Genovese was stabbed to death in the middle of the night while 38 of her neighbors listened from the safety of their apartments. Although the victim screamed for help and her assailant took almost 30 minutes to kill her, no one even reported the incident to the police, never mind fighting off Genovese's killer.

Social scientists of the day argued that this apparent indifference was a result of what they called "diffusion of responsibility." That is, although they may have been concerned for the victim, Genovese's neighbors also felt a lack of personal responsibility to intervene. They reasoned, "Why should I risk my neck when there are other witnesses who will surely come to the rescue?"

However it was explained at the time, the Genovese case was the first nationally recognized episode of bystander apathy—one of the most distasteful by-products of the American preoccupation with spectatorship. Although it was first acknowledged then, however, bystander apathy is a phenomenon not peculiar to the 1960s; nor is it exclusive to any one generation of people. Just by going through recent newspaper stories, it would not be difficult to argue that people still do not help one another.

Take the Manchester, New Hampshire woman who was brutally raped in a yard just steps away from her apartment. Apparently, she was in full view of several of her neighbors but they ignored her pleas for help. In Raleigh, North Carolina, a motorcyclist injured in an accident lay face down on a crowded highway and counted 900 cars over a 3-hour period before anyone stopped to assist him. In Boston, a third-year medical student was jumped by four teenagers while riding his bicycle home from the hospital. Many people watched, but none of them intervened. In New York City, a group of jeering and joking youths watched while a 30-year-old man was electrocuted on the third rail of the subway station at Times Square. And on and on.

Observers of the social scene have used such cases in arguing for the existence of a destructive and callous side of human nature. Based in part on the writings of Freud and, more recently, of ethnologists such as Konrad Lorenz who emphasize the evolutionary basis for aggressive behavior, they have focused on bystander apathy to illustrate how people are moving away from one another. This point of view is sometimes so thoroughly one-sided, however, that it ignores the fact that altruism is a value in virtually all human societies and forms the basis for most of the world's great religions. Americans have long institutionalized altruism by awarding medals for outstanding acts of selfless heroism as, for example, in the medals awarded by the Carnegie Hero Fund Commission or, during wartime, in the U.S. Armed Forces' awarding of the Congressional Medal of Honor.

While some observers dwell on the seedier side of human nature, hundreds of others donate one of their kidneys for transplantation into another human being. Thousands more have donated their blood at some personal expense and inconvenience. And millions regularly donate money to their favorite charities.

Today, more than 30 years after the Genovese case, these acts of generosity and selflessness seem more abundant than ever. In addition, there seems to be less tolerance for those individuals who respond to others with indifference or selfishness. In fact, bystander apathy seems fast becoming the exception to what may be a new norm of social life: being willing to risk inconvenience, embarrassment, and even personal safety to come to the rescue of the victims of crimes and accidents. The evidence is, at this point, admittedly anecdotal and informal, but it is nonetheless highly suggestive. There have been numerous reports recently of acts of great heroism and courage performed by average citizens who haven't otherwise stood apart as paragons of virtue. The members of this breed of Good Samaritan are very serious about taking personal responsibility for the plight of others, refusing to take refuge in the anonymity of the crowd or the masses.

We used to see purse snatchers and muggers; now we also see bystanders who chase and catch the mugger. We used to read about physicians who drive past automobile accidents because of the fear of a lawsuit; now we also read about doctors who come to the rescue of accident victims and, in the process, may suffer injuries of their own. We used to see corruption in government and industry; now we also see "whistle-blowers" who risk being fired to expose practices that they believe to be dangerous to the public.

An example of personal altruism is the behavior of Lennie Skutnik, the young man who was honored by former President Reagan in 1982 for his heroic rescue of a survivor of an Air Florida crash in the icy waters of the Potomac River.

In 1986, Richard Young, a New York City fireman, risked serious injury to rescue a total stranger—a truck driver who hung by his arms from the steering wheel of the cab of his truck as it dangled over the edge of a bridge. Arriving on the scene, Young threw himself under the truck driver's body to break his fall. In saving the man's life, Young received a broken leg, a broken ankle, and severe back injuries.

In 1992, a small plane crashed into a small, ice-covered pond, injuring its student pilot and his flight instructor. The duo might have died were it not for the heroic efforts of two passersby who rushed out to the sinking plane and rescued the two with a ladder they had laid on the ice. One of the rescuers, David Leal, suffered a dislocated shoulder and hypothermia in the process.

In 1994, 15-year-old Razeena Sadiq was on her way to school when she spotted an apartment building in flames. Without regard for her own safety, Sadiq raced into the burning building four times—at one point crawling on her hands and knees through the smoke-filled corridors—to guide 13 residents to safety. Afterward, she gave her coat to a half-naked man whom she had rescued and then pounded on doors until she found him a place to escape the early-morning cold.

In 1997, 53-year-old Harvey Randolph saw his neighbor Jill Fitzgerald being viciously attacked and bitten by four pit bulls. The 155-pound plumbing contractor rushed to Jill's side, where he was finally able to drag her to safety. The brutal attack left Jill with 113 wounds to her head, neck, back, arm, and legs, requiring 188 stitches. Harvey suffered an injury to his elbow, requiring surgery, and wounds to his hands and right leg.

What characteristics distinguish these Good Samaritans from the rest of humanity? Social scientists have discovered that individuals who intervene in a dangerous situation are likely to have had training in first aid, lifesaving, or police work. In addition, they tend to be exceptionally tall and heavy. These attributes, won through training and strength, give them the sense of competence or efficiency they need to be willing to inject themselves into potentially hazardous situations. Good Samaritans also tend to be adventurous types who have taken other risks with their personal safety.

The most important conditions accounting for the rise of the Good Samaritan may be found in the types of heroes they choose to emulate. Researchers have discovered a common factor among German Christians who, during World War II, helped rescue the victims of their Nazi persecutors; civil rights activists of the 1950s and 1960s (called Freedom Riders); and altruistic children: the presence of someone to serve as a model of altruism. In the case of a child, that model is likely to be an intensely moralistic parent with whom the Good Samaritan can closely identify. In adults, models for appropriate behavior are also found in the national heroes they choose to emulate.

On the national level, we continue to have our idols of consumption—those bigger-than-life images on the screen, tube, or field of play whose accomplishments fill our leisure hours with music, comedy, and drama. But there is now a new breed of national hero as well. Today, we have idols of activism—individuals who are admired and revered not for their ability to keep us entertained but for their courage to take active charge of their own lives and the lives of others. In the face of overwhelming and impersonal social, political, and economic forces, such as the threat of nuclear war, big government, and corporate mergers, we feel increasing admiration for those who come forward from their place among the spectators. This change in our culture may have made heroes out of the likes of Oliver North, Bernard Goetz, the Guardian Angels, Sylvester Stallone as Rambo and Rocky, Dustin Hoffman in the film *Hero,* Harrison Ford in *Air Force One,* Kate Winslet in *Titanic,* and Jeff Bridges in *Fearless,* but it has still made us admire the courage of Lennie Skutnik and Razeena Sadiq. ∎

# We Are in the Midst of a Cultural Revolution
(And We Don't Even Know It)

FBI statistics released over the last few years offer some good news to those Americans who have been afraid to walk the streets after dark or to do their shopping downtown. Believe it or not, the murder rate has been dramatically down in most of our major cities.

Part of the explanation is demographic. The 76 million baby boomers have matured into middle age and out of the violence-prone age group. Rather than commit murder and aggravated assault, they have graduated into such lower-risk white collar offenses as fraud and embezzlement.

Another factor involves a beefed-up criminal justice system. In New York City and Houston, Texas, for example, zero-tolerance policing has taken more and more offenders off the streets so they cannot reach innocent victims. New York's former Police Commissioner William Bratton has attributed the success of his crime-fighting efforts to a get-tough policy that locks away street criminals long *before* they have had the opportunity to commit serious offenses.

But the most important factor in declining murder rates in our major cities may have nothing to do with population or prisons. Whether we realize it or not, we are presently in the early stage of a cultural revolution. Americans everywhere, at the grassroots level and up, are just beginning to recognize that they can make *the* difference in the crime rate. In response to severe cutbacks by state and federal government, they are working to repair the moral, social, and economic damage done to our youngsters and to take the glamour out of destructive behavior.

Fed up with crime, ordinary citizens are enthusiastically addressing the issue of violent crime and, in the process, are re-defining it. Everywhere you look, you find groups and organizations focusing on violence in conferences, lectures, keynote speeches, and workshops. Taking their cue from growing popular sentiment, local institutions have sponsored a number of impressive programs aimed at local youngsters—for example, gun-buyback programs, midnight basketball, conflict resolution and mentoring programs in the schools, scholarships for local residents, summer jobs and after-school activities sponsored by local companies.

Parallels can be found in our changing attitudes toward cigarette smoking. Prior to the Surgeon General's report in 1968, smoking was widely regarded as fashionable and stylish. But more than 25 years later, the campaign has discredited smoking and stigmatized smokers. Hopefully, the same may soon happen to individuals who have a propensity for violence.

Of course, although the anti-smoking campaign reduced the consumption of cigarettes among adults, it essentially failed to convert young people. In 1996, for example, an additional 4000 teenagers continued to take up the smoking habit every day.

In the same way, teenagers aren't likely to be touched by a cultural revolution that asks that they become less violent and destructive. Many youngsters don't think about long-term consequences—whether about contracting lung cancer or going to prison. Indeed, teenagers are likely to feel invincible and therefore immune from the impact of their own violent behavior.

Unlike anti-smoking campaigns, however, the cultural revolution in attitudes toward violence is being aimed not at teenagers at all, but directly at their parents, their teachers, their clergy, their neighbors—at adult members of society who are (or should be) responsible for dealing with teenagers. This is important because our youngsters will change only to the extent that society's response to them changes first.

Years ago, researchers conducted a famous study which examined the effect of illumination on the productivity of a group of factory workers at a company known as Western Electric. First, researchers turned up the lights and worker productivity increased. Then, researchers turned down the lights to approximate pale moonlight, but productivity increased even more. Their conclusion was surprising: Degree of illumination had nothing to do with productivity; it was actually a result of the increased attention these workers were given by the researchers. Participating in an "important" experiment had made the workers feel special. Researchers called their unexpected finding the Hawthorne Effect because of the area in which it was located.

We are in need of nothing less than a Hawthorne Effect in the area of juvenile violence. Teenagers who have been routinely ignored, unsupervised, and left to fend for themselves must discover that their parents and teachers care. Youngsters who join gangs and carry weapons to school must be guided and counseled more and more by clergy and social workers. For the first time in their young lives, they will feel important and special, because somebody besides a drug dealer cares about them. ■

# Elevator Culture
## You Really Can't Do Anything Else but Stare at the Door

Social psychologists conducted an experiment in which they gave elevator riders at Ohio State University an opportunity to help themselves to a coupon good for a complimentary Quarter Pounder with cheese. After entering the elevator, riders saw a poster reading "Free McDonald's Burger" and a pocket underneath it in which coupons for one Quarter Pounder were located. All they had to do was take one.

Fifty-six people entered the elevator alone. Of this number, 26 were randomly permitted to ride without other passengers, while 16 rode with one other passenger and 14 rode with two other passengers (all of the other "passengers" were really confederates of the experimenters who decided on a random basis whether subjects rode with 2, 1, or no other riders).

Results obtained in this experiment showed that individuals riding alone were much more likely to help themselves to a coupon for a cheeseburger than were riders in the presence of other passengers. In fact, of those individuals riding by themselves, 81% took a free coupon. With one other passenger present, however, only 38% took a coupon; and with two other passengers present, only 14% helped themselves to a coupon.

Why would elevator passengers avoid doing something to their advantage—taking a coupon for a free cheeseburger—just because other riders were present? The answer seems to involve the influence of *elevator culture*—a set of unspoken, unwritten rules of behavior that is widely shared and generally observed by people in elevators who ride with other passengers. The riders in this experiment were eager to avoid doing something that might call attention to themselves in the public setting of the elevator, even if it meant sacrificing a free fast-food lunch. They didn't want to be deviant; they desired to avoid being embarrassed; they didn't want to look different.

Actually, there isn't very much you can do that is right in an elevator, especially if you are among strangers. Almost all of the rules of elevator riding seem to be *proscriptive*—things you are definitely not supposed to do. The only prescriptive—positive—rule involves standing quietly while facing the elevator door, and that is precisely what most passengers will do. Unless they want to be regarded as weirdos, most riders avoid talking to anyone they don't know, staring at anyone, touching anyone, even breathing on anyone (they wouldn't want to violate the personal space of other riders, even in a crowded elevator).

One interesting thing about elevator culture is that it extends far beyond the elevator walls. Actually, almost any public setting—whether walking on the streets of a city, eating in a restaurant, or sitting in the park—carries a set of rules that severely limit the quality and quantity of social interaction: In all of these places, there is little, if any, talking to, touching, or even looking at strangers. As a result, strangers in a big city who are physically close might as well be miles apart, as far as interaction is concerned.

Of course, individuals also have some control over their culture; they don't have to passively conform to it. In an early study of conformity, Solomon Asch (1952) studied a group of eight people, in a classroom situation, who were asked to match the length of a line drawn on the blackboard with one of three comparison lines drawn on an index card. All judgments were made out loud and in order of seating in the room. Actually, only one participant in the Asch study was a naive subject, and he voiced his judgment after hearing several other students state theirs first. (These others were confederates of Asch who had been instructed to respond incorrectly when asked to match the length of the lines.)

Over a number of trials with different groups, approximately one third of the naive subjects made incorrect estimates in the direction of the inaccurate majority—in other words, about one in three conformed. But when a lone dissenter gave support to the naive subject by going against the majority judgment, the rate of conformity dropped dramatically to less than 6%.

Thus, if even one person waiting in line for a table in a restaurant starts talking to other customers, he or she might serve as a role model for other customers to imitate. Who knows, maybe lots of people will take a chance and get involved in the conversation. And if one rider in a crowded elevator has the courage to take a coupon for a free cheeseburger, everybody might conceivably end up having lunch on McDonald's. ■

■ **FOCUS** *Suggestions for Further Reading*

Many of the ideas and evidence found in "The Immaculate Americans" were based on Gale Largey and David Watson's excellent 1972 article "The Sociology of Odors," in the *American Journal of Sociology*. In this article, Largey and Watson make a very strong case that olfactory sensitivities vary from culture to culture. The use of images of odor to discredit a group of people is only one form of dehumanization. For a fascinating examination of this phenomenon, see Sam Keen's *Faces of the Enemy: Reflections of the Hostile Imagination* (1986).

Evidence for the tremendous influence of "Baby Boomers: A Generation Without a Gap" can be found in *Great Expectations: America and the Baby Boom Generation* (1980), by Landon Y. Jones. To focus specifically on women at the leading edge of the baby boom generation, I recommend Winifred Breines's excellent book *Young, White, and Miserable: Growing Up Female in the Fifties* (1992). For a cultural-materialist view of social customs more generally, read Marvin Harris's fascinating work, *Cultural Materialism* (1979). Harris suggests that the variety of cultural behavior around the world is a result of the adaptations that societies make to their particular environments. For example, in 1487, the Aztecs suffered from a profound shortage of animal protein in their diet; they were not able to raise cattle, sheep, goats, horses, pigs, or llamas. In response, they continued to incorporate cannibalism into their warfare. After a battle, they would eat their enemies—thousands of them—as an alternative source of animal protein.

The trend toward activist cultural heroes as introduced in "The Demise of Bystander Apathy" is beginning to show up in the sociological literature. For example, Myron Peretz Glazer and Penina Migdal Glazer, in their important book *The Whistleblowers: Exposing Corruption in Government and Industry* (1989), have studied the growing phenomenon of ethical resisters—those courageous workers who expose corruption in high places. Despite harassment and a strong possibility of defeat, these whistle-blowers operate out of a sense of moral responsibility to challenge the status quo. If you are interested in learning more about altruism and empathy in everyday life, read Alfie Kohn's book, *The Brighter Side of Human Nature* (1990). He convincingly presents evidence from sociology, psychology, and biology to suggest that human beings are more caring and generous than we give ourselves credit for. According to Kohn, helping others occurs as often as hurting others. Samuel Oliner and Pearl Oliner's penetrating work *The Altruistic Personality* (1988) examines hundreds of individuals who helped rescue victims of the Nazis during Hitler's reign of power. The Oliners emphasize that the rescuers had a deep-rooted empathy for other people's problems that they developed in their childhood homes. Their parents were profoundly moral individuals who often acted on their beliefs; in our terms, they were everyday versions of idols of activism.

A work by Robert Bellah, Richard Madsen, William Sullivan, Ann Swidler, and Steven Tipton, *Habits of the Heart: Individualism and Commitment in American Life* (1985), analyzes both the tradition and the direction of our cultural values. According to Bellah et al., we have lost touch with our cultural commitment to community in favor of a preoccupation with rugged individualism. In the process, we have ignored the very traditions that might help us today.

We have apparently also ignored our children. Rates of youth violence can be examined in a report to the United States Attorney General on rates of juvenile offending in *Trends in Juvenile Violence* (1996) by James Alan Fox. For an analysis of the role of firearms in juvenile crime, see Alfred Blumstein's (1995) report "Violence by Young People: Why the Deadly Nexus?" An expanded version of the argument I make in the snapshot concerning a cultural revolution in our thinking about teenagers can be found in the winter, 1998 issue of the *Mid-Western Educational Researcher*. ■

## ■ DEVELOPING IDEAS  *About Culture*

1. Writing topic: Name five of your heroes from fields such as business, sports, entertainment, religion, and politics or from everyday life. Then write an essay in which you identify the particular cultural values reflected in their heroic accomplish-

ments. To start, consider whether they are idols of production, consumption, or activism.

2. Writing topic: We have seen how much cultural clout the baby boomers have had in American society. Thinking about music, art, comedy, and television, identify some of the contributions that your generation has made to American popular culture.

3. Research topic: Have Americans' attitudes toward children and teenagers really changed in any important way? To address this question, select several issues of a leading general-interest magazine that has published for decades (for example, *Reader's Digest*). Choose several issues from a very recent period (say, 6 months of issues from 1998) and from the same period a couple of decades ago (say, 6 months of issues from 1978). Compare the magazine for these two time periods in terms of the percentage of all articles devoted to exploring issues related to children and teenagers. Were more articles about children printed in the 1998 issues? Also, examine the qualitative differences between periods of time. In 1978, what issues or problems did most of the articles about youngsters discuss? How did those issues or problems differ from the ones addressed in 1998 articles?

4. Research topic: Let's say you were a sociologist who was studying the culture of your campus. Construct a one-page questionnaire to identify some of the values and practices that are widely shared among the students at your college. Then give the questionnaire to a sample of students. (To get at how values operate in everyday life, you might want to ask questions such as how many hours a week your respondents spend doing things like studying, partying, watching TV, and so on. You might also ask them to rank order certain activities—getting good grades, having a date, being well liked, making lots of money—in terms of how important they are.)

5. Research topic: Pick up a recent issue of a supermarket tabloid—preferably the *National Enquirer* or the *Star*. Analyze all of the profiles in that issue with respect to the human qualities and problems that they emphasize. First, determine how many profiles feature celebrities. How many of these are entertainers, business leaders, or politicians? How many would you regard

as idols of consumption? Next, find out how many profiles feature ordinary people who do extraordinary things. How many were Good Samaritans? How many performed miracles or great acts of courage? How many would you regard as idols of activism? ■

# PART TWO

## Socialization

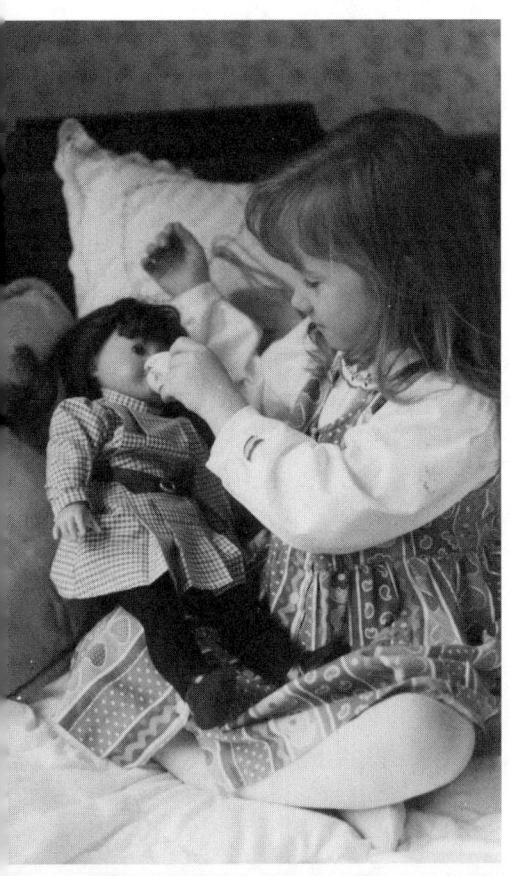

How do we get to be you and me? From our toys and play--boys with trucks and girls with baby dolls--we learn to act according to prescribed roles. In addition to toys today, television is another agent of socialization. But what exactly is it encouraging us to be?

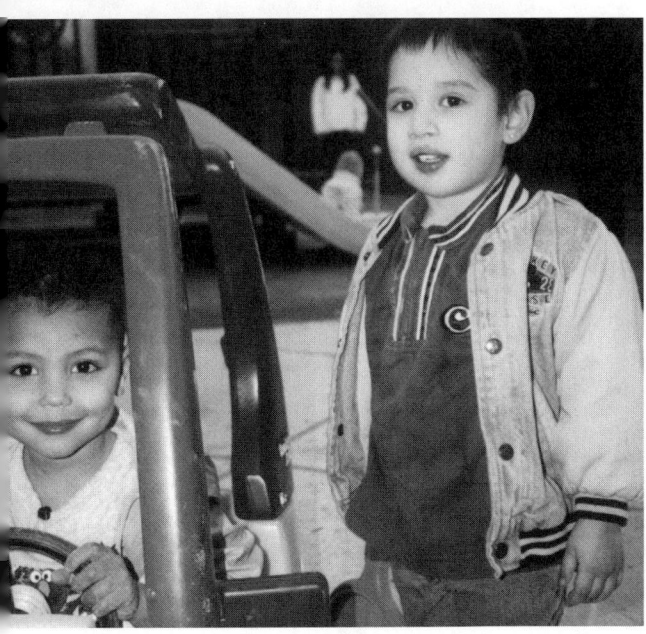

**I**t was a disquieting scene: three African Americans waiting for a bus, and, across the road, a young white child—he couldn't have been more than 2 or 3 years old—shouting racial slurs at the top of his lungs as he took bites from a Three Musketeers bar. Just as the trio got aboard the bus, the boy's mother rushed over, picked him up, and carried him away. At first, she was furious that he had left her side without asking permission. But then she smiled as he continued to yell "nigger" and point in the direction of the bus as it sped away.

Just like the child at the bus stop, we aren't born knowing the content of our culture; we learn it. We absorb our culture—we learn love of country, motherhood, apple pie, and racism through a process of interacting with others—parents, teachers, friends, television characters—that we call *socialization*.

Much socialization is, by necessity, somewhat parochial. Few of us grow up with a representative sample of life experiences. So, many Americans don't realize, for example, that Caucasians are a minority among the world's racial groupings or that Christianity is a minority religion worldwide. They believe, incorrectly, that most of the world looks like they and their family and their friends look.

In "Teaching Students They Are Not at the Center of the Universe," my colleague Will Holton and I discuss a course that we developed to help change our students' views of people who are different with respect to race, religion, and ethnic background. The effect of any distortions in our perception may be profound: Many of the decisions we make in everyday life are in part a result of what we believe the world to be like. If, for example, we exaggerate the likelihood of being a victim of violence, we might decide to carry a handgun. If we overestimate the wealth of our nation, we may oppose programs that aid the homeless. And if we incorrectly believe that most of the members of another race or ethnic group are rapists and murderers, we might avoid them like the plague.

Socialization is absolutely essential for individuals to become humanized members of their society. Without internalizing culture, we would all be "sociopaths," essentially unsocialized individuals who lack conscience, human warmth, and empathy for the problems of other people. Yet just because individuals accept the values and norms of their group doesn't necessarily mean that they will automatically reject violence. Indeed, even the most brutal, most repulsive behaviors have been taught during the normal course of socialization.

A good deal of socialization occurs at school, where a child typically spends much of the day with teachers, classmates, friends, and counselors. Sadly, there is also far too much violence in the school environment, even at the elementary level. In response, principals have instituted programs and policies that aim at resolving dangerous conflicts and teaching students techniques for preventing any future acts of violence. But administrators don't always recognize the need for after-school activities—sports, music, drama, student government, and so on—to provide alienated and unsupervised youngsters with a safe alternative to violence. Especially in the elementary years—kindergarten through fifth grade—such programs are usually missing. And even where after-school activities exist at the middle and high school levels, they are generally treated as a privilege for the "good" students rather than as a cost-effective violence-prevention program in which all students learn values and establish models for healthy relationships.

Any discussion of the way in which values are transmitted to the members of American society would be incomplete if it failed to include a discussion of the mass media. In particular, television has an immense influence as an *agent of socialization*, if for no other reason than that the average child spends 4 to 5 hours daily in front of the tube. I often hear concerned Americans voice their criticism of television for what it supposedly does to children. And much of this criticism is well deserved. But let's put the effect of television in perspective: There is far less street crime in Japan, yet Japanese television is even more violent than ours. Why? Perhaps because few Japanese parents use television as a baby-sitter. Instead, they sit *with their children while they watch the tube,* ready to monitor, interpret, and discuss. It isn't so much that American television is so strong but that our other institutions—family, business, religion, and schools—aren't doing their part that may be at the heart of the problems we now face.

Socialization does not come to an abrupt end just because someone grows up. To some degree, adults continue to change throughout life, and they, too, are very much influenced by what they watch on the tube. "Confessions of a Soap Opera Addict" suggests that the fantasy on TV is often seen as the reality. In the extreme case, soap opera characters become our "good friends." We may even send them gifts. In "Adult Socialization Can Be Murder," I examine an extreme example of development into adulthood gone awry—the case of murderers who don't start killing until they reach their 30s, 40s, or even 50s. I ask, if early childhood is really the critical factor, why didn't these killers begin their murder sprees when they were 12 or 18 or 24? Why did they wait until they were middle-aged adults?

To some extent, most Americans share an overall way of life. They accept at least some values and practices from the dominant culture as their own. At the same time, Americans are not rubber stamps of one another. Just as they share in the dominant culture, their worldviews are also colored by their being members of a subculture—a group whose members have their own peculiar set of values, objects, and practices. In "Sticks and Stones May Break..." we see the importance of membership in subcultures for establishing an individual's personal identity. The question "Who am I?" is often answered in subcultural terms: "I am Irish American," "I am Latin American," and so forth. These subcultural names are important in symbolic terms for their ability to express the shared consciousness and pride of a group in society whose members may struggle with their subcultural identity.

Charles Horton Cooley, writing at the turn of the century, suggested that our self-image is developed through the "looking-glass process." That is, we form a sense of self by interacting with others. In this process, we come to make a judgment of our self—that we are smart, attractive, moral, and so forth—based on the judgments that others make of us. Thus, the other people in our lives are, in a sense, a mirror in which we see our own reflection. Cooley called the result of this process the "looking-glass self."

If self-esteem develops in social interaction, then names can hurt you as much as sticks and stones. In "Sticks and Stones May Break..." we see that children who are given unpopular or unusual names may be treated in a negative way. In response, they develop poor self-esteem and actually behave as predicted: badly. The entire process becomes a "self-fulfilling prophecy."

When applied to a group of people, names often contain a cultural *stereotype*—an unflattering image that the members of a society learn from their parents, teachers, friends, and the mass media. The racial slur "nigger" shouted by the toddler in the bus stop scene that opened this section is "only" a name. But it contains one of the nastiest cultural stereotypes ever taught to our children.

The importance of the self can hardly be exaggerated. According to the California Task Force to Promote Self-Esteem and Personal and Social Responsibility (and see also Mecca, Smelser, and Vasconcellos, 1989), self-esteem is a "primary factor" affecting how well an individual functions in society. Many, if not most, of our major social problems, the California Task Force contends, originate in low self-esteem. It should be emphasized, at the same time, that the chain of cause and effect runs both ways—that self-esteem itself is affected very much by an individual's involvement in such social problems as poverty, domestic violence, and educational inequality. ■

# Teaching Students They Are Not at the Center of the Universe
## We Construct the World in Our Own Image
*with Wilfred Holton*

Segregation is a fact of life on college campuses around the country. Visit a crowded cafeteria at almost any college or university, even the most diverse, and you will see students of a "feather" sitting and eating together—whites with whites, blacks with blacks, Latinos with Latinos, and Asians with Asians. Even worse, when college students from diverse backgrounds occasionally interact, they often do so under hostile conditions. A recent survey of 550 colleges conducted by *U.S. News & World Report* found that, over a 1-year period, 71% of the campuses in the United States had at least one hate incident involving a student's race or religion.

Of course, it's not just college students who opt for spending quality time with their "own kind." Americans of all ages and backgrounds tend to separate themselves by race and religion in almost every aspect of daily life.

It is not surprising that our beliefs about other human beings are often inaccurate, based more on stereotype than reality. A person who grows up in Boston may come to believe that 60% of all Americans are Catholic because that is what she sees on her street, at her workplace, and in school (the real figure is more like 20% of all Americans). Similarly, someone raised in Washington, DC may be convinced that 70% of all Americans are black (the real figure is approximately 13%); a New Yorker might swear that half of all Americans are Jewish (the real figure is close to 2%). We tend to apply what we see every day to what we don't see every day.

And television is not very helpful in giving its viewers an accurate portrayal of the entire range of humanity. Communication research conducted for more than a decade indicates that heavy television viewers tend to overestimate the percentage of the world population that is white and male and underestimate the amount of poverty in our country. They are socialized to accept a false view of social reality because this is precisely what they see on TV every evening beginning at 8 p.m. The world of prime-time television is overpopulated by white males who possess more than their share of wealth and power. F. Earle Barcus, in his work *Images of Life on Children's Television: Sex Roles, Minorities, and Families* (1983), discovered that the same could be said of children's television—of the 1,145 characters appearing on 20 children's programs, only 42 were black and 47 belonged to some other minority group.

Last fall, we teamed up to teach an experimental sociology course that took teams of undergraduate students out of the traditional classroom to provide service to the local community. Yet the emphasis of the course was on changing students, not changing the neighbors. Our objective was to broaden students' perspectives—to give them an opportunity to interact with people of different races, ethnicities, or religions, and to do so in a spirit of cooperation, civility, and good will. In short, we hoped to challenge and clarify our students' views of social reality, with the objective of preparing them to live in an increasingly diverse world.

One of the important functions of formal education is to broaden our personal experience, to serve as an agent of socialization with aspects of life that we might otherwise never experience firsthand. And this is precisely why a formal course that combines classroom instruction with firsthand involvement in the life of the community makes so much sense, at least theoretically.

Based on the quality of their personal essays and academic transcripts, 17 undergraduate students were selected to participate in our course. The majority was white, but black, Asian, and Latino students were represented as well. Every week, each student in the course performed 5 hours of community service; the students then met together as a class for 2 hours to discuss issues related to the way that groups interact. Our text was Ruth Sidel's *Battling Bias*, an analysis of diversity on campus. In addition, students wrote logs summarizing their community service experiences for the week and a more inclusive term paper at the end of the quarter. Our final class meeting together consisted of oral team presentations in which students summarized their community experiences and reflected on how those experiences had changed their own feelings and thinking about diversity.

The range of student reactions was as broad and varied as their agency placements. Some reported initially feeling out of place when exposed to an unfamiliar situation in which they were, for the first time ever, the "racial minority." For example, Sally, a white student from a middle-class Boston suburb, helped with peer-mediated conflict resolution with girls at a local high school where most of the young people were either black or Latino. At first, she regarded the students as "nameless girls who frightened me in the hallways." About one girl who had gotten into a fist fight, Sally later remarked, "During our first meeting, I didn't think she wanted me in the room. Now, six weeks later, she calls me her 'big sis' and confides in me." Sally reports that her experience caused her "to look at people in a very different light" and to be "more sensitive to issues of racial, class and social disputes." As a result, she has decided to continue working at the school for the entire year and is applying to graduate school to study juvenile crime.

Other students in our course discovered unexpected civility among the community members they served. Richard, a young man from upstate New York, conducted empathy training as part of a conflict resolution program with racially diverse first-graders at an elementary school near Chinatown. Richard's experience changed his perspective. "Perhaps the biggest thing I noticed in working with these kids was just how little race differences matter to them," Richard suggested. "It is not that they don't understand that other people have different skin colors than they do, it's that they don't care. It made it so obvious to me that racial hatred is a learned thing."

Some of our students learned a good deal from being part of a project team whose members were diverse. For example, Marjorie, a biracial student who grew up in a part of Maine where there was only a tiny Jewish population, had been exposed to many anti-Jewish stereotypes. But through her partnership in a Cambridge agency with a Jewish woman from New York, she felt comfortable enough to ask her about her religion. Toward the end of the course, Marjorie remarked, "Now that I possess a better understanding of the Jewish faith and background, I am less likely to believe the stereotypes employed to discredit Jewish individuals."

However, not every student left the course with an increased sense of optimism or tolerance. Some were stunned by the depth and pervasiveness of the problems confronting members of the community, especially those who are impoverished. Jamie, a student who worked with battered women at a local hospital emergency room, explained that she was "overwhelmed by the difficulty in ever making wide, far-reaching gains combating this huge problem, yet I am left wanting to help more. It was amazing for me to see how common domestic violence is. . . . I was also struck, however, by the strength some women possessed in surviving tremendous difficulties. It is a shame their strength is wasted on situations they shouldn't have to face."

Because they have grown up shielded from those who are different, many young people lack the skills necessary for good citizenship, tolerance, civility, and humanitarianism. They need to be made aware of the existence of poverty and homelessness, flaws in the criminal justice system, prejudice and discrimination, and their own mortality. Most of all, college students need to learn that they are not at the center of the universe. As one of our students concluded after spending 10 weeks working with Boston teenagers, "The greatest content of learning in this course was about myself. I was forced to explore my own prejudices and those of others like me." ∎

# Confessions of a Soap Opera Addict
The Daytime Serials Are More Than I Bargained For

I've been watching *Days of Our Lives* each day of my life for more than 25 years. It all started when I took a year off to finish my doctoral dissertation. Each afternoon, my wife and I sat together in the living room of our small apartment: She watched soap operas; I wrote my thesis. Working at home was tough enough, and eavesdropping on midday melodrama didn't help. In fact, it only reinforced my long-held impression that soaps were at about the same intellectual level as Saturday morning cartoons, but these, at least, had action. Did anyone really care whether Julie and David got together again, when Marie would discover that her fiancé was actually her long-lost brother, or whether Missy was pregnant with another man's child?

I didn't think so. Soap operas were television's "opiate of the masses," I had decided: that medium through which too many Americans vicariously escaped their dreary existence into the make-believe world of the rich and beautiful. While the pressing economic and social problems of our society went ignored, millions of *General Hospital* groupies became Luke and Laura, if only for a few minutes a day. They needed that soap opera "fix" to make their lives seem exciting and worthwhile. America's daytime serial fanatics were being distracted from improving their own lives by a particularly insidious form of fantasy and escapism.

I was especially annoyed by the depiction of women. They seemed always to be getting pregnant, not for the purpose of having children but to manipulate and control the men in their lives. They used pregnancy to trap boyfriends into unwanted marriages or husbands into maintaining unwanted marriages. In addition, any woman who dared have a career in a field traditionally dominated by men—medicine, law, business—was either mentally ill or evil. The sex role socialization message was unmistakable: Women were to stay out of the boardrooms and executive offices and stay in the kitchens and bedrooms "where they belonged."

It occurred to me that, in some perverse way, soap operas were a mass form of socializing young people to accept the status quo. Even while college students of the 1980s were scheduling or skipping courses to accommodate *General Hospital,* the majority of daytime serial watchers were high school graduates who had never attended college, mostly middle-aged women. Many used the characters on soaps as role models for how to handle their spouses. But what they learned frightened me: first, that infidelity and promiscuity were acceptable, even desirable, modes of sexual behavior; second, that divorce was the answer to any difference, no matter how trivial. If your marriage wasn't smooth as glass, get a divorce. Or a lover. Better yet, get a lover, then a divorce.

By the third or fourth week of watching out of the corner of my eye, I noticed something peculiar was happening to me. If I had to be away during a weekday afternoon, I'd call home for a rundown of that day's episodes. I scheduled meetings with colleagues so I wouldn't miss a particular serial. It got to the point where my wife would have to tear me away from *my* show to take a phone call or answer the door. It was painful to admit, but I was hooked. I was brainwashed. I had become a socialized "soapie."

Perhaps as a sort of therapy, I spent a good part of the next few years immersed in the study of soap operas. It was legitimate: I was teaching a course in mass communication, and my students were discussing the impact of television on society. I read what the experts—psychologists, sociologists, and assorted communications specialists—had to say. I even assigned student projects to analyze the characters on daytime serials.

Surprising, to me at least, was their conclusion that soap operas were much better than prime-time dramatic series in representing women, minorities, and older people in central roles. While young and middle-aged males were vastly overrepresented on prime-time television, in soap operas one half of the characters were women. Even more to their credit, soap operas featured actors and actresses who remained on the show for decades. Many of them aged gracefully and remained thoroughly attractive, while they continued to play roles central to the plot. Indeed, older people were treated much better on soap operas than on most other television fare. And the daytime serials frequently focused on a range of social problems: intergroup conflict, juvenile delinquency, alcoholism, organized crime—issues that were all but ignored by soaps' prime-time counterparts.

It was soon clear to me why soaps are so appealing to so many. For one, they provide us with the things we find lacking in modern life. Monday through Friday, without fail (barring an occasional hijacking or a presidential news conference), we follow our "good friends" into their offices, living rooms, and bedrooms. We attend Carey and Austin's wedding and Peter's funeral, visit Roman in the hospital after surgery or Susan after childbirth. We watch Sammie argue with her mother-in-law, John make love with Marlena, and Stephano fake his reformation. We often get to know more about the personal lives of our favorite soap opera characters than we know about our real neighbors. In an era of anonymity, soap operas give us intimacy. Sadly, for those who are socially isolated, this may be the one and only source of intimacy in their lives, but perhaps this is better than nothing.

Soap operas make us feel good about ourselves. Misery loves miserable company, and our own problems are somehow less painful when we're able to compare them with the troubles of those we admire. The world of the daytime serial is the world of the wealthy, beautiful, and powerful—our cultural heroes, the people we aspire to become. Yet these characters have problems with their families and friends, much worse than ours. So we feel better, at their expense, of course.

Soap opera intimacy often takes the form of snooping, but only in the most positive sense. By eavesdropping, we're given the opportunity to rehearse our own emotional reactions to problems that may confront us in everyday life. Observing untimely deaths, kidnappings, divorces, and mental illness on television, we learn something about the manner in which we might handle similar problems in our own lives.

At least part of the influence of daytime serials can be attributed to the credibility of television as a form of mass communication. Study after study shows that Americans trust the authenticity of the images they see on the tube. In the process, however, heavy viewers often develop a distorted view of social reality. They tend to exaggerate, for example, the amount of violence they are likely to encounter in everyday life, the proportion of criminal cases that end in a jury trial, and the likelihood that physicians will perform miracle cures. For these viewers, the fantasy world on television becomes the reality. During the 5 years that Robert Young played Dr. Marcus Welby, the actor received more than 250,000 letters asking him for medical advice. Admiring fans were apparently unable to distinguish actor Young from character Welby.

This incredible power of soap operas as an agent of socialization was brought home to me several years ago when I met some of the actors on *Days of Our Lives*. As an interested observer, I couldn't resist asking them the questions that might confirm what I always suspected: Do soap opera addicts confuse the fantasy world of the daytime serials with the real world in which they live? Yes—and often. Whenever a *Days of Our Lives* star either gives birth (it's only a pillow), gets married (a rhinestone wedding ring), or dies (usually a failure to renegotiate the actor's contract), cards and gifts appear at the studio, they said.

For me, soaps have a special appeal. As a sociologist, I investigate problems that have no easy solutions. I spend years studying serial killers, for example, and am troubled that we can't predict from childhood experience who will eventually commit hideous crimes. I research the causes of prejudice and discrimination and still see the number of racist acts of vandalism and desecration increasing. And like others, I see criminals too often get suspended sentences while their victims suffer; the rich get richer as homelessness grows; and the questionable ethics of politicians go unpunished.

And that's how soaps are different. Warm, friendly, predictable, they make sure people get what they deserve. ■

# Violence in City Schools
## What Principals Are Doing to Stem the Rising Tide
*with Heather Beth Johnson*

Last year, 64% of elementary school principals in five Massachusetts cities—Boston, Springfield, Worcester, Lowell, and New Bedford—suspended or expelled violent students. At the high school and middle school levels, this figure was close to 96%. In eight public schools, 26 or more students were dismissed for carrying weapons or being violent.

The good news is these city schools offer a wide array of programs and activities aimed at preventing or resolving violent student behavior. Conflict resolution programs are extremely popular in elementary, middle, and high schools. In addition, especially in the high and middle schools, there are peer-mediation programs, programs to combat hatred and racism, and community volunteers to serve as tutors and mentors.

However, while after-school programs such as intra-mural athletics, drama, art, music, and student government are offered by 90% of the high schools and 96% of the middle schools, only 14% of the elementary schools sponsor such programs.

The virtual absence of after-school activities in kindergarten through fifth grade leaves many younger children without opportunities for wholesome experiences and activities in the afternoons. Because they generally do not begin until the middle-school years, supervised activities after school have not become part of the students' daily routine and therefore may not be seen as "cool" or "hip" by the students who most need them. By the time such programs are available, students have already entered adolescence and may be unwilling to participate in activities supervised by adults, especially by teachers and parents.

Although most urban high schools and middle schools provide at least some after-school activities, such programs are usually restricted to students who are in academic good standing, haven't been troublesome in the classroom, have economic resources, and can find transportation home. In 95% of the schools offering after-school activities, one or more restrictions are placed on the students' eligibility to participate. As a result, students most lacking in healthy alternatives after classes end—those who are impoverished, alienated, and idle—are less likely to participate.

According to school principals, a major reason why so many schools impose eligibility requirements for participating in after-school activities involves a lack of economic resources. Such programs are vastly underfunded.

But another reason has to do with the manner in which such activities are defined by the administrators themselves, who fail to recognize after-school programs as violence or conflict prevention measures. They are much more likely to view such activities as a *privilege* extended to *deserving* students—those who are achievement oriented, compliant, and well-behaved.

More than 40% of all violent crimes committed by teenagers occur between 2 p.m. and 7 p.m. Yet, today, 57% of all juveniles lack full-time parental supervision; they grow up in dual-career families or in single-parent households.

In wealthy communities, many children may be provided with opportunities for healthy after-school alternatives. In areas where economic and human resources are seriously lacking, however, children tend to be on their own until their parents come home from work.

Therefore, expanding the school day to include *all* students in after-school programs would structure our youngsters' days so that their time could be spent on worthwhile activities. What we currently regard as after-school programs should be incorporated into a longer school day during which traditional academics become interspersed among clubs, internships, athletic programs, job apprenticeships, and the arts. By restructuring the school experience so that it is identified with more than academic subjects, the meaning of school would be broadened to include appealing and practical activities from the youngsters' standpoint.

Such an approach requires making a major investment—one that ought to be shared by a wide range of local interests and institutions. The cost would be heavy, but not so heavy in human terms as our continuing disinvestment in our children and their future. Some 135,000 U.S. teenagers go to school each day carrying a firearm. It would be a step in the right direction if they traded in their weapons for softball gloves, tennis rackets, and art supplies. ■

# Sticks and Stones May Break...
In Reality, Names May Indeed Hurt You

What's in a name? Plenty, if you happen to be political spokesperson Larry Speakes, Professor Robert Smart, psychiatrist Ronald Bliss, or District Court Judge Darrell Outlaw. Whether or not such names inspired career choices, they undoubtedly have provided material for countless after-dinner conversations. Can't you imagine Dr. Bliss being ribbed about teaming with Dr. Ruth for a late-night advice show?

According to psychologist Ron Harré and his associates at the State University of New York at Binghamton, and confirmed in countless other studies, the influence of names begins in childhood. Names that we are familiar with—common names, such as John and Michael—are associated with images of strength and competence, whereas unusual names, such as Ivan and Horace, conjure up weakness and passivity. Consequently, those kids who are unfortunate enough to have been given bizarre or unpopular names are sometimes poorly adjusted and pessimistic about their prospects of being successful in the future; they tend to score lower on achievement tests and get lower grades in school.

This phenomenon extends into adulthood. Men who have strange or unusual names are more likely to suffer from mental illness or to have criminal records. In many cases, a *self-fulfilling prophecy* may operate during the socialization process. A child is ridiculed because of his name. As a result, he develops a negative attitude toward himself that influences his behavior in the classroom and on the playground. And teachers and peers notice this poor behavior. They assume that kids with unusual names aren't very competent or skillful. So very little is seen, very little is expected, and very little is obtained.

The importance of names is nowhere more important than in Hollywood. Consider all the celebrities who weren't born with the right name for the image they want to portray. The former William Bailey is now Axl Rose, Alphonso D'Abrusso is Alan Alda, Robert Zimmerman calls himself Bob Dylan, Frances Gumm's stage name was Judy Garland, and Patricia Andrzejewski is better known as singer Pat Benatar.

The flip side of this is that uncommon names sometimes imply uniqueness. One might speculate that Zsa Zsa Gabor, Ya Hoo Serious, River Phoenix, Doug E. Doug, Moon Zappa, Pee Wee Herman, The Artist Formerly Known as Prince, Yakov Smirnoff, Rip Torn, Whoopi Goldberg, Madonna, and Mr. T owe at least part of their celebrity status to their names.

Minority groups are also painfully aware of the power of a name to socialize its members to failure and negative self-esteem. People of color prefer to be called *black* or *African American.* They reject labels such as *colored* and *Negro,* contending that these were long ago assigned to them by outsiders. Jesse Jackson recently called for the elimination of the black label in favor of a group identity such as *Afro-American* that would emphasize an African cultural heritage in the same way that white ethnic groups—Irish Americans, Polish Americans and Italian Americans—choose to stress their European ancestry. Even the term *minority* may be falling out of favor, as more and more people of color refuse to see themselves as playing a minor role in American society. Similarly, many women now resent being labeled *girls, babes,* and *chicks* because of the infantilized image. And older Americans tell survey researchers that they like being called *senior citizens* rather than *aged* or *elderly,* indicating that old age continues to be a difficult situation for millions.

People who possess a physical disability have often been victimized by harmful and misleading names. Given the negative connotation of the word *cripple,* it is clear why they seek to avoid being referred to in this way. But even the word *handicapped* is not always appropriate, deriving its meaning from an earlier period in which individuals with physical disabilities were forced to the streets, to beg, literally, cap in hand. There are numerous individuals today—blind, deaf, in wheelchairs, and on crutches—who actively seek to maximize their independence and who prefer not being labeled as handicapped.

By characterizing the entire person, the word *disabled* completely ignores the possibility that an individual might possess strengths as well as weaknesses. Yet very few persons are actually disabled in the absolute sense; most possess certain disabilities, some more severe than others, but they also have abilities that can be nurtured and developed if they are not overlooked. A paraplegic may never be able to run in the New York Marathon without the help of a wheelchair, but he or she may still become a brilliant lawyer or physician.

The symbolism in name-calling makes it just as dangerous as sticks and stones. Thousands change the name that appears on their birth certificate; thousands more drop an offensive middle name or use a nickname to avoid the negative attention provided by the formal version of their name. For minority groups, the painful history represented by a label often becomes part and parcel of the consciousness-raising rhetoric of their causes. Socialization counts a great deal: To accept the name is regarded as accepting the stereotyped image that group members have worked so hard to modify or overcome. Under such circumstances, the word may not be the thing, but it certainly has an effect that means the most—an individual or group's identity.

Whoever suggested that names will never hurt you must have been named John or Judy or maybe even Robert. It is doubtful that Horace or Eugene would have agreed. ∎

# Adult Socialization Can Be Murder
Development Continues Throughout Life

Everything we have learned about the process of socialization suggests that what happens to us while we are very young is extremely important for shaping the rest of our lives. Suffering a horrible experience at the tender age of 2 can leave us with a lifelong phobia. Losing a loved one at 4 or 5 can contribute to making an individual into an emotionally needy adult. Failing the sixth grade can affect our self-image, even many years later.

Yet while early childhood may be critical, we must not forget that development continues throughout life. To focus only on the first few years in the biography of an individual may be to ignore some of the most influential aspects of his or her development.

Erik Erikson, for example, who was a student of Sigmund Freud and a famous theorist in his own right, proposed that the close personal relationships that are formed by an individual during young adulthood help determine a sense of intimacy. According to Erikson (1950), if such relationships are not successfully established, the individual will suffer a profound sense of isolation. What is more, in midlife (between the ages of 30 and 50), a failure to master the challenges of work and raising a family can result in an individual's coming to a nonproductive, egocentric sense of self.

To understand what can happen when adult socialization fails, we might examine its most extreme, most deadly consequences. It is interesting to note that most mass murderers—those who massacre large numbers of people—don't kill until they are middle-aged men, in their 30s, 40s, or even 50s. James Huberty, for example, who massacred 21 people, mostly Hispanic children, at a San Ysidro McDonald's, was 41; George Hennard, who opened fire in a Killeen, Texas cafeteria, killing 23, was 35; and R. Gene Simmons, who exterminated 14 members of his family in Russellville, Arkansas, was 46. If early childhood had been the critical factor, then these killers would probably have expressed their murderous impulses much earlier in life—say, by the time they were in their teens or early 20s.

Many mass killers do have profound problems growing up. They may have been abused, neglected, or even abandoned. But so have hundreds of thousands—perhaps even millions—of people who never kill anyone and who never will. The determining factor in the process of creating a mass murderer seems to reside in what happens to a killer when he attempts to make the transition into adulthood or even later. Does he have adequate support systems in place—family, friends, and neighbors—to get him through the tough times, to encourage and support him when he loses a job or an important relationship? Or is he set adrift to fend for himself in an unfamiliar and unfriendly world of anomie? In Erik Erikson's terms, does he suffer a profound sense of isolation at the very time in his life that he needs social support?

Also relevant is whether mass killers are successful at home and at work. Actually, most of them have suffered a number of losses in important areas of life—for example, the loss of a close relationship by separation or divorce or a profound financial loss through being fired or terminated. In Erikson's terms, having failed to master the challenges of work and raising a family, they feel a profound sense of stagnation. James Huberty, after losing his job, moved from a small town in Ohio to a suburb of San Diego. After settling in California, he again became unemployed. This time, however, his family and friends were back home in Ohio. He didn't have anyone to give him the psychological boost that he so much needed.

What happens (or fails to happen) in the biography of a mass murderer may give us clues as to what can be done to prevent violence in general, even when committed by otherwise unremarkable members of society. Of course, it would be wonderful if we were able to intervene in the early childhood of every individual who is in trouble. But we must also not ignore those troubled young people who are already in their teen years and beyond early intervention.

The majority of adult offenders do have a juvenile record, but the majority of teenagers with a juvenile record do not later become criminals. Many adolescents who commit deviant acts when they are 14 wouldn't dream of committing the same crimes when they reach 24 or 25. Just because we cannot reach troubled youngsters during the first few years doesn't mean that we should give up on them later. On the contrary, if Erikson is right, then we should be doing everything possible to help such teenagers over the obstacles of developing into adults so that they can become productive citizens. In the process, we might even prevent a mass murder. ■

■ **FOCUS** *Suggestions for Further Reading*

As suggested in "Sticks and Stones May Break . . . ," labeling children with an unpopular name can sometimes become the basis for a self-fulfilling prophecy. They are expected to perform poorly, treated accordingly, and eventually come to perform as expected. Of course, names can also have a positive effect. In a recent article, Rebekah Fowler and Ann Fuehrer (1997) interview five women who kept their last names after marriage. For all five, retaining their names was an important way to maintain their autonomy as individuals and to assert their equality in marriage.

For a discussion of the looking-glass self, you might read Charles H. Cooley (1902). I would, however, suggest that you first read the work of George Herbert Mead, a University of Chicago social philosopher whose insights into the development of the self continue to provide major direction for sociological research. Particularly germane is his discussion of *role taking*—the process whereby an individual learns to take another person's point of view. By means of role taking, children come to define themselves in the way that significant others (for example, mother and father) view them. If Mommy and Daddy see a child as stupid, the child will come to see herself as stupid; if parents see a child as lazy, then he will develop a self-image as someone who is lazy. Try *Mind, Self and Society* (1934). It's difficult reading (Mead's students compiled this work from their notes) but completely worthwhile. To see what labeling can do to students' performance, read the modern classic by Robert Rosenthal and Lenore Jacobson, *Pygmalion in the Classroom* (1968). Rosenthal and Jacobson told teachers that certain of their students were "bloomers" based on their high IQs. Actually, the so-called bloomers had been chosen at random, and their IQs were no higher than those of students not labeled as bloomers—at least at the beginning of the study. By the end of the year, however, the IQ scores of bloomers were significantly higher than they had been when they entered the class. Apparently, the expectation given to teachers ("These students are superior") was enough to make the labeled children perform at a higher level.

For an excellent summary of research relating self-esteem to chronic social problems, such as child abuse, educational failure, alcohol and drug abuse, welfare dependency, and violent crime, read *The Social Importance of Self-Esteem* (1989), edited by Andrew

Mecca, Neil Smelser, and John Vasconcellos. You might be surprised to discover just how much self-image contributes to the really big problems of our day. At the same time, poor self-esteem itself does not develop in a social vacuum; instead, it often develops out of our most difficult social problems, including job displacement, abuse, and educational failure. The relationship between self-esteem and social problems therefore represents a vicious cycle that becomes difficult to break. Where do you intervene? In *Resocialization: An American Experiment* (1973), Daniel Kennedy and August Kerber describe their efforts at resocializing individuals who "don't fit in." Such resocialization programs—compensatory education, criminal rehabilitation, and training for the hard-core unemployed—all assume that it is possible to intervene to alter an individual's attitudes, values, and abilities.

In "Teaching Students They Are Not at the Center of the Universe," my colleague Will Holton and I discuss a course that we developed to help modify our students' views of people who are different with respect to race, religion, and ethnic background. The course takes as a given that few of us grow up with a representative slice of personal experiences and that each of us is, in a sense, forced to construct our own version of reality. This, of course, leads to distortion and misunderstanding. To see how such factors play out on college campuses around the country, read Ruth Sidel's excellent work, *Battling Bias* (1994). To read more about the changing situation of diversity on campus, see Howard J. Ehrlich's *Campus Ethnoviolence and the Policy Options* (1990). For a detailed analysis of violence against lesbians and gays, read the range of articles contained in Gregory Herek and Kevin Berrill's reader, *Hate Crimes: Confronting Violence Against Lesbians and Gay Men* (1992). Gary D. Comstock's *Violence Against Lesbians and Gay Men* (1991) provides research data and many interesting insights. One is worth repeating here: Whereas attacks against the members of different races are usually committed by economically marginal teenagers, violence against gays seems to come from every socioeconomic level.

For a student-oriented collection of readings about the production and construction of reality, see Peter Kollock and Jodi O'Brien's *The Production of Reality* (1994). Concerning the effect of television in this process, see George Gerbner, Larry Gross, Michael Morgan, and Nancy Signorielli, "Charting the Mainstream: Television's Contributions to Political Orientations," in the *Journal of Communication* (1982). In addition, Charles R. Wright, in *Mass Communication: A Sociological Perspective* (1986), discusses the manner in which television cultivates a distorted view of reality.

Concerning "Confessions of a Soap Opera Addict," there is plenty of data about the daytime serials in *The Soap Opera* (1983) by Muriel Cantor and Susanne Pingree. For a more general treatment of socialization and mass communication, there are many excellent articles in Sandra Ball-Rokeach and Muriel Cantor's *Media, Audience, and Social Structure* (1986). A recent study of sex roles and soap operas by Mary Strom Larson (1996) looks at the disparity between television portrayals and reality—in this case, the reality of single motherhood. Larson found that viewers perceive that most single mothers are like those they see everyday on *Days of Our Lives*—they have good jobs, healthy babies, are well-educated, and are not poor.

In "Violence Goes to School," Heather Johnson and I present evidence to suggest that after-school programs are missing, especially from elementary schools, and that such activities might have an important impact on the reduction of dangerous conflict and violence. Of course, school violence is often treated with formal social control (law enforcement) responses such as metal detectors and police security. According to P. A. Noguera (1995) in the *Harvard Educational Review,* however, efforts to socialize youngsters to a less violent alternative can be much more effective than any law enforcement strategy. Rather than send in a police force, it may be more effective to send grandparents as mentors and tutors and role models.

To understand more about the factors in adulthood that contribute to criminality, read Robert Sampson and John Laub's insightful study, *Crime in the Making: Pathways and Turning Points Through Life* (1994). Sociologists interested in how people are influenced during adulthood have paid a good deal of attention to career socialization—how individuals come to adapt the practices and values of their work experiences. In a classic study, Howard Becker and his colleagues attended medical school classes with regular students to observe the lessons that aspiring physicians were being taught as part of their medical training. The researchers determined that the idealistic and humanitarian views of first-year medical students gradually faded and were replaced by a more practical view of medical knowledge and practice. See *Boys in White* (1961), by Howard S. Becker, Blanche Geer, Everett C. Hughes, and Amselm L. Strauss. More recently, Robert Granfield attended classes at a prestigious northeastern law school to determine how law students were being socialized to their careers as attorneys. Not unlike what Becker and his associates had discovered concerning medical students, Granfield found that many law students abandoned their idealism in favor of a more cynical form of "thinking like a lawyer." Granfield published his results in "Legal Education as Corporate Ideology," in *Sociological Forum* (1986). ■

## ■ DEVELOPING IDEAS  *About Socialization*

1. Research topic: Test your knowledge of "social geography." In writing, estimate the percentage of students at your college (or your city)—from 0% to 100%—who are from foreign countries; who are African American, Asian American, and Latin American; and who are women. Now, find a source that can give you an accurate count—the library, the registrar's office, city hall, and so on. How close were your estimates to the actual percentages?

2. Research topic: Communication researchers suggest that television is fixated on appealing to young and wealthy American men, those who buy sponsors' products. As a result, commercial TV does not portray the elderly, minorities, and women as they really are. In fact, many of these groups are virtually absent from the tube. Analyze one episode of any prime-time dramatic series. In writing, identify the race, ethnic identity, gender, and approximate age (child, teenager, young adult, middle-aged, or old) of each major character. If possible, also find each major character's occupation and social class (from their job, house, car, and so on). If an alien from Mars knew nothing about American society except for what she learned from this one episode, what would she likely conclude about the makeup of the United States?

3. Research topic: Most sociologists believe that the self arises out of social interaction. Cooley's looking-glass self includes this idea. To apply this notion on a personal level, try the following "experiment" suggested by Manford Kuhn's measure of self-

analyzing your friend's answers, consider how many relate the self to other people: group memberships (fraternity member, sister, son, and so on) or categories (Catholic, Protestant, American, female, and so on). Kuhn says that children tend to define themselves in very specific terms. For example, they might say they are "nice to a sister" or "good at playing cards." Adults tend to define themselves in much more abstract terms—groups or categories of human beings. If you want to learn more about Kuhn's Twenty-Statements Test, see his 1960 article "Self-Attitudes by Age, Sex, and Professional Training."

4. Writing topic: There is a good deal of evidence that socialization continues throughout life. Robert Granfield and Howard Becker both suggest that students become less idealistic as they are trained formally for a career either in law or medicine. Thinking about these studies as they might apply to your own behavior and attitudes, write an essay in which you play the role of participant-observer to discuss how your personal values and aspirations might have changed as a result of your classroom experiences. Since you first began taking courses at the college level, have you become more or less idealistic in terms of your career objectives? If you have changed, exactly what do you believe to be responsible for that change? Does your major have something to do with it? Do you ever feel that your instructors are giving you a subtle, perhaps implicit, message about what is important and what is not important in a career, in life? What have you learned from your classmates in this regard?

5. Research topic: Locate a group of several elementary school students—preferably from the same classroom—who are willing to discuss with you any problems involving conflict, violence, and harassment at their school. (Make sure that you have the permission of their parents before you actually begin. In fact, it might be wise to have parents in the room when you talk with their children.) Come to the session prepared with a list of open-ended questions regarding how often they see weapons, what types of weapons they have seen, how teachers and administrators respond to students who carry weapons, how safe they feel at school versus their own neighborhood, what they do after school, whether they are alone—lacking in adult supervision—after school, how often they see violence at school,

after school, whether they are alone—lacking in adult supervision—after school, how often they see violence at school, what types of violence—hair-pulling, punching, stabbing, choking, and so on—they have witnessed, whether they have been involved in a violent confrontation, and so on. ∎

# PART THREE

## The Group Experience

If two's company, three or more is a group. Groups can be either unwanted crowds of others or gatherings of families and friends. Although groups differ dramatically from small and intimate--like the toddlers in the wagon--to mob-like and alienating--like a university commencement exercise--they all provide the social context for our interaction with one another.

I've lived in the same house since 1976, and I don't even know my next-door neighbor. It's not that I can't remember his name (though I can't). It's that I don't even know what he looks like. Well, I *didn't* know, until the other day. I was standing alone in a train station in Boston, when a complete stranger walked up to me and said, "Aren't you Jack Levin?"

I, of course, nodded my head and asked him politely how he knew me. He told me his name and then informed me that he was my next door neighbor. When I asked him how long he had lived next door, he responded, "For 5 years." Shocked and embarrassed, I welcomed him to the neighborhood. Well, what else was I to do?

The amazing thing is that I live in a middle-class suburb—not in a city apartment, but in a single-family house on a quiet residential street with other single-family houses. Another amazing thing is that I really like people, including my neighbors. But most of my friends and group memberships are somehow associated either with my job or with my family. There seems to be very little room left over in my everyday interaction for the people on my block.

And, then, there is the assumption—perhaps unwarranted—that most of my neighbors are not any different than I am. They have their own lives, too—they are away during the day, probably belong to various organizations at work, probably have a circle of friends and family with whom they share their leisure hours. What kind of an effort have they made to get to know me, I ask? (Boy, am I defensive!)

This section is about the experience of being in groups, ranging from families, roommates, neighbors, and peers, on the informal side of the continuum, to the largest organizations—companies, universities, government agencies—you might possibly envision, on the more formal side. *A group provides the social context for interaction between people*—two or more individuals who are aware of one another's presence and who adjust their behavior toward one another. They may talk, laugh, cry, work, play, scream, fight, debate, struggle, or cooperate—but, always, together. This interaction is the essence of the group experience. It is also the essence of what sociologists study.

In our mass society, there are people who have little more than superficial contacts with other human beings. Some have no informal contacts at all. However, while the old, traditional forms of social interaction represented by family and neighborhood may have weakened, they have been replaced by new patterns of interaction. As suggested in "College Fraternities: A Counteracting Force on Campus," students may depend a good deal on fraternities and sororities to find others to date and to develop lasting friendships.

In addition to fraternities and sororities, there also seem to be growing numbers of unconventional groups called "cults." Sociologists have always defined cults as loosely structured and unconventional forms of religious groups whose members are held together by a charismatic leader who mobilizes their loyalty around some new religious cause—typically a cause that is at odds with that of more conventional religious institutions. Using this definition, almost any new religious group that hasn't yet become institutionalized—whether benign or dangerous—could be regarded as a cult. From a sociological perspective, then, early Christianity during Roman times was a cult, but so were the Branch Davidians under David Koresh. Of course, the term *cult* has recently been used much more broadly to include any group—whether religious or not—that may be dangerous or destructive.

Some people need an excuse just to gather together with others. In "Reunion, American Style," we discover Robert Merton's term *latent function*. He recognized that many of our social arrangements have not only a formal purpose but also an unintended and unrecognized consequence. Professional conferences, for example, frequently held on an annual basis, provide an opportunity for practitioners to exchange information in formal sessions. But the latent, and therefore unintended, unrecognized effect may be even more important. In bars, restaurants, and hotel lobbies, participants from around the country reunite to chat. Their informal conversations often provide the basis for exchanging ideas and collaborating on projects. In the same article, we see the manner in which patterns of behavior can become institutionalized. That is, aspects of the social order become widely accepted and organized. In our society, class reunions have become big business, a commercial success.

Speaking of big business and big organizations, "Children of the Organization Men" takes a look at two generations: first, those men (there were very few women who did this) who came of age in the 1950s and worked for most of their careers in large organizations. What happened to their children? Did they become organization men and women? Or did they choose to follow a different career path for themselves? A recent study of organizational offspring indicates that their fathers' loyalty to corporations and conformity to social order were hardly passed on to the next generation. Instead, the sons and daughters of organization men turned their attention to the self and cherished raw individualism. ∎

# College Fraternities: A Counteracting Force on Campus
Where Else Would Students Get to Know One Another?

Those who long for a return to a time of strong family ties, neighborliness, and a simpler life often invoke the term *mass society* to characterize a long-standing trend in American society that they deplore. The image of mass society is all too familiar to millions of Americans in the 1990s—people who feel very much alone, city dwellers and suburbanites living in "boxes," dissatisfied customers who talk on the phone to automated voices, rush-hour traffic that won't quit, and waiting lines a mile long.

All of these forms of mass society are, indeed, a painful fact of life for millions of Americans. Yet at the same time that older types of social relations have diminished, they have been replaced by new, and sometimes deceptively effective, forms of intimacy and informality that compensate for the loss of traditional primary ties and counteract feelings of loneliness and isolation.

Technology has provided some degree of compensation. Even when friends and relatives are physically separated, they can still sustain primary contacts by telephone. Or as a postmodern form of social interaction, they can keep in touch by means of personal computer (the Internet, e-mail, and electronic bulletin boards), even if they are thousands of miles apart.

Of course, technological devices such as long-distance telephones and computers hardly make up for the eclipse of community in America. Their essentially superficial forms of interaction cannot possibly compensate totally for the loss of profound friendship and family networks found in the neighborhoods or communities of another era.

This can be seen clearly in the case of millions of college students around the country who leave their families—perhaps for the first time ever—to take up residence on a campus, sometimes located thousands of miles from home. It should come as no surprise that these students, especially if they are on large and diverse campuses, often search for opportunities for intimacy and friendship. Some find the primary contacts they need in fraternities and sororities.

Membership in college fraternities and sororities seems to ebb and flow, depending on the social circumstances surrounding campus life at a particular point in time. In 1966, some 30% of all college students belonged to Greek-letter societies; by 1976, however, this figure had dropped to only 19% nationally. In fact, fully two thirds of these colleges had experienced declining fraternity enrollments. During the 1970s, on some campuses across the country, fraternities completely disappeared.

Apparently, the fraternity's ability to counteract mass society on campus was overruled, at least during this period of time, by a more powerful theme among the college-bound baby boomer generation. Many college students of the early 1970s regarded fraternity membership as thoroughly inconsistent with their interests in civil rights, student rights, antiwar activism, feminism, racial equality, and independence from institutional constraints.

James A. Fox and I conducted a study showing that the disappearance of college fraternities was short-lived. By examining the fraternity and sorority membership figures around the country, we discovered a major resurgence of interest in campus fraternities. By 1981, almost one half of all colleges and universities had already reported seeing growth in fraternity enrollments. As more and more students sought structured opportunities to meet other students, date, and develop friendships, the fraternity began to make its big comeback. Especially on campuses where most of the students came from outside of the immediate area, there were few commuters, and there was little else to attract students in the wider community, fraternity membership thrived and prospered. In some southern schools, fraternity membership reached 80%.

In a mass society, independence can be very lonely. For college students who miss the intimacy of family life, fraternities and sororities provide a new set of "brothers" and "sisters" and a home away from home. ■

# The Appeal of Cults
If You Can't Get What You Need From Your Friends, You May Be Tempted to Join

What in the world is a cult, anyway? And how do you know it when you see one? Are we talking about Heaven's Gate and the dozens of people who in 1997 committed mass suicide so they could reunite on a spaceship? Or the more than 80 Branch Davidians who perished at Waco, after their compound was stormed by federal agents? How about Jonestown, Guyana? In 1978, 912 people died there, because their leader Jim Jones urged them to sip cyanide-laced KoolAid. Should we include transcendental meditators? Members of the Divine Light Mission? The Unification Church and Scientology, even though these groups have millions of members around the world? How about the Charles Manson "family"? In 1969, several Manson members killed seven innocent people.

Of course, many people nowadays use the term "cult" to refer to any new group they dislike—whether its members are organized around religion, race, flying saucers, psychotherapy, politics, or self-improvement. The despised cults are typically accused of engaging in devious practices. It is suggested, for example, that some of their members recruit in a deceptive way—they might, for example, lure unsuspecting students by promising them a free-of-charge get-together at some retreat, while they fail to inform the students of their true intent. Other cults are said to use methods of mind control or thought reform (a.k.a. brainwashing) for transforming their recruits into totally obedient zealots. According to this view, members of cults become dependent on an authoritarian group leader who claims to have some special knowledge, gift, or talent. In extreme cases, recruits are no longer allowed to make any important personal decisions without consulting their leader and must give up all relationships with old friends and family. Finally, it is said that the most dangerous of such cults have coerced their members into committing suicide, murder, or both.

Every once in awhile, the behavior of a cult confirms the worst suspicions of its detractors. On March 26, 1997, for example, 39 members of the Heaven's Gate cult committed mass suicide in their rented mansion in Rancho Santa Fe near San Diego. Marshall Applewhite, the cult's leader, had convinced his followers—20 women and 19 men ranging in age from 26 to 72—that a spaceship traveling behind the Hale-Bopp comet was coming to pick them all up, just as soon as they could shed their "vehicles" or "containers" (also known as bodies). They were totally convinced that civilization on Earth was about to end but that they could enter a higher life form by killing themselves and then boarding a spaceship for what they called "the next level." So, as instructed by their leader, they took poison and—just in case—placed plastic bags over their heads to asphyxiate themselves.

Not only did the Heaven's Gate suicide victims represent both genders and a wide range of ages, they also consisted of blacks, Latinos, and whites who had come from all over the country. And these were not stupid, crazy, or uneducated people—they were computer skilled, musically talented, and scholarly—but they were also needy, lonely, and depressed. Many had abandoned their families and friends months or years earlier.

It is right, of course, to be concerned for the lives of people who are down on their luck when they are recruited by dangerous or deceptive cults. When someone has suffered a profound loss or has no place to turn for guidance and support, he or she is particularly vulnerable to the attempts of groups, dangerous or not, to influence his or her decisions through conformity and obedience to authority.

At the same time, it is pure myth to suggest that recruits typically lack any power to resist while under the spell of a madman. Even vulnerable individuals possess an *active self*—they are typically not brainwashed into misbehaving, but comply willingly with the requirements imposed on their membership. From this viewpoint, there is a definite limit to the power of a charismatic leader to mold or shape the behavior and beliefs of his disciples. Most cult leaders are not in the category of a Jim Jones or Marshall Applewhite, even if they are extremely persuasive.

Over the past 20 years, there may have been as many as 20 million Americans involved for varying periods of time in some kind of cult. The reason why such groups have widespread appeal is that they provide precisely what many Americans find lacking in their everyday lives—a sense of belonging and friendship, a feeling of power, control, and importance, and a more general sense of structure and certainty.

At various times in our lives, all of us can fall into vulnerable states—we may be lonely, hurting, having a hard time socially, having academic problems, or feeling overwhelmed or confused. During such temporary periods of misery and loss—for whatever reason—another person can have more influence over us than during other periods of time. If the members of a cult come along and promise to show us the way out of our misery, then we may very well be tempted to join them. If, however, we can instead count for a helping hand on our instructors, advisors, friends, clergy, resident assistants, family, and counselors, then the most persuasive cult will seem totally irrelevant. ■

# Reunion, American Style
The Ritual of Recommuning

In her novel of the same name, Rona Jaffe suggests that a class reunion "is more than a sentimental journey. It is also a way of answering the question that lies at the back of nearly all our minds. Did they do better than I?"

Jaffe's observation may be misplaced but not completely lost. According to a study conducted by social psychologist Jack Sparacino, the overwhelming majority who attend reunions aren't there invidiously to compare their recent accomplishments with those of their former classmates. Instead, they hope, primarily, to relive their earlier successes.

Certainly, a few return to show their former classmates how well they have done; others enjoy observing the changes that have occurred in their classmates (but not always in themselves, of course). But the majority who attend their class reunions do so to relive the good times they remember having when they were younger. In his study, Sparacino found that, as high school students, attendees had been more popular, more often regarded as attractive, and more involved in extracurricular activities than those classmates who chose not to attend. For those who turned up at their reunions, then, the old times were also the good times!

It would appear that Americans have a special fondness for reunions, judging by their prevalence. Major league baseball players, fraternity members, veterans groups, high school and college graduates, and former Boy Scouts all hold reunions on a regular basis. In addition, family reunions frequently attract blood relatives from faraway places who spend considerable money and time to reunite.

Actually, in their affection for reuniting with friends, family, or colleagues, Americans are probably no different from any other people, except that Americans have created a mind-boggling number and variety of *institutionalized* forms of gatherings to facilitate the satisfaction of this desire. Indeed, reunions have increasingly become formal events that are organized on a regular basis, and, in the process, they have also become *big business*.

Shell Norris of Class Reunion, Inc., says that Chicago alone has 1,500 high school reunions each year. A conservative estimate on the national level would be 10,000 annually. At one time, all high school reunions were organized by volunteers, usually female homemakers. In the last few years, however, as more and more women have entered the labor force, alumni reunions are increasingly being planned by specialized companies rather than by part-time volunteers.

The first college reunion was held by the alumni of Yale University in 1792. Graduates of Pennsylvania, Princeton, Stanford, and Brown followed suit. And by the end of the 19th century, most 4-year institutions were holding alumni reunions.

According to Paul Chewning, vice president for alumni administration at the Council for Advancement and Support of Education (CASE), the variety of college reunions is impressive. At Princeton, alumni parade through the town wearing their class uniforms and singing the praises of their alma mater. At Marietta College, they gather for a dinner dance on a steamship cruising the Ohio River. At Dartmouth, alumni act as lecturers and panelists in continuing education courses for their former classmates.

Clearly, the thought of cruising on a steamship or marching through the streets is usually not, by itself, sufficient reason for large numbers of alumni to return to campus. Chewning contends that alumni who decide to attend their reunions share a common identity based on the years they spent together as undergraduates. For this reason, universities that somehow establish a common bond—for example, because they are relatively small or especially prestigious—tend to draw substantial numbers of their alumni to reunions. In an effort to enhance this common identity, larger colleges and universities frequently build their class reunions on participation in smaller units, such as departments or schools. Or they encourage affinity reunions for groups of former cheerleaders, editors, fraternity members, musicians, members of military organizations on campus, and the like.

Of course, not every alumnus is fond of his or her alma mater. Michelle Favreault, Associate Director of Alumni Affairs at Brandeis University, suggests that students who graduated during the late 1960s may be especially reluctant to get involved in alumni events. They were part of the generation that conducted sit-ins and teach-ins directed at university administrators, protested Reserve Officers' Training Corps (ROTC) and military recruitment on campus, and marched against "establishment politics." If this generation has a common identity, it may fall outside of their university ties—or even be hostile to them. Even as they enter their middle years, alumni who continue to hold unpleasant memories of college during this period may not wish to attend class reunions.

Not all reunions are school affairs. People also reunite as an unintended consequence, a latent function of gatherings designed for other reasons. Hundreds of professional associations hold annual conferences or conventions to keep their members up-to-date with developments in their fields. Yet many of the professionals who attend pass up the formal sessions—the speeches and seminars—in favor of meeting informally in bars and hotel lobbies with colleagues from other cities and states.

Attendees are given an excuse to swap experiences with friends they haven't seen since the last meeting. Similarly, the manifest function—the intended and recognized purpose—of wedding ceremonies is to unite the bride and groom in matrimony. Yet weddings (as well as funerals, confirmations, and bar mitzvahs) also serve an important latent function: They provide occasions for scattered families and friends to reunite.

The poignancy of these meetings suggests a more general principle: If reunions make people cry, it is not, as Rona Jaffe proposes, because they have come out on the short end of things *now*. It is because they measured up so well 20 years ago, and they want to relive the good old days with tears of joy. ∎

# Children of the Organization Men
## The New Individualists

For more than 30 years, William H. Whyte's *The Organization Man* was the most widely read book about organizational life. Focusing on middle-class Americans at mid-century, Whyte argued that bureaucratic organizations actually shaped almost every aspect of our lives. They dictated that employees be "groupminded." That is, they were expected to be flexible to the demands of others, to be completely loyal to the corporation, and to remain uncommitted to a set of values. In this view, organizations rewarded only those individuals who were "good team players." Nothing else really counted, from the corporate point of view.

In collecting data for his book, Whyte followed his organization men (this is not a sexist slight; there simply weren't any organization women) into their offices, but he also visited their suburban homes, schools, and neighborhoods. He interviewed their wives and observed their children.

Whyte's description of the social role of the corporate wife is particularly telling. Any employee who aspired to be promoted to an executive position needed a wife who obeyed the corporate rules. She had to be willing to make frequent moves from city to city for the sake of her husband's job, to assume exclusive responsibility for household chores and child rearing, and to stay away from her husband's workplace. She must never gossip about the office with other corporate wives, never get drunk at a company party, never be too friendly with the wives of other employees whom her husband might pass on his way up the corporate ladder, and never show up her husband by being superior to him in any way.

Whyte observed the rise of a pervasive *social ethic*—a widely held belief that the group was the essential source of creativity and that "belongingness" was *the* basic human need. Thus, the demand for "yes-men," "happy homemakers," "family togetherness," and "team players." Hence, the worship of the organization.

For their book *The New Individualists: The Generation After the Organization Man,* Paul Leinberger (whose father was an organization man interviewed 30 years earlier by William Whyte) and Bruce

Tucker recently interviewed the sons and daughters of the original organization men as well as hundreds of other "organizational offspring." They focused on baby boomer Americans—those men and women born between 1946 and 1964 whose fathers had worked for most of their careers in large organizations. Included in their study were "the middle manager chafing at the slow progress up the promotional ladder, the forest ranger dreaming of writing novels, the aging hippie getting by on marginal jobs, the gypsy scholar in today's brutal academic job market, the entrepreneur starting a software company, the corporate star rising rapidly, and the free-lance consultant seeking autonomy."

Leinberger and Tucker found that the organizational offspring were very different from their fathers in terms of outlook, values, and motives. Children of organization men resembled one another with respect to attitude toward organizations, style of interpersonal relations, and patterns of consumption. But unlike their fathers, all of them were strong individualists. Whereas organization men admired the salesman, their offspring admire the artist. Whereas organization men were conspicuous consumers, their children cherish creativity. Whereas organization men were dominated by sociability, their offspring pursue self-fulfillment.

Leinberger and Tucker suggest that social change is partially responsible for the new norms embraced by organizational offspring. During the past 30 years, we have seen major changes in the conditions of work, leisure, economics, family life, and politics. The huge number of acquisitions and mergers in the late 1980s makes a lie of the concept of corporate loyalty; many longtime executives were summarily dismissed without any cause other than a need to reduce corporate expenses. The dual-career family introduces competing sources of allegiance between work and home. Foreign competition and reduced profits put new strains on American business.

The resulting generational differences are often profound. As soon as they finished school, organization men married, went to work, and began having children. By their mid-30s, the last of their 2 or 3 children was born. By contrast, children of the organization men often remain in school through their 20s, marry even later, and are in their 30s when they have their 1.8 children.

An obsession with the self can be observed as a major element in the individualism of the organizational offspring. At home, in schools, and through the mass media, the members of this generation were urged to enhance "self-expression," "self-fulfillment," "self-actualization," "self-assertion," "self-understanding," and "self-acceptance." Just as surely as their parents accepted a social ethic, the children of the organization men developed a *self ethic*.

The organization men were severely criticized for their almost robotlike obedience to corporate aspirations. But their children's individualistic ideal has also come under attack. According to Leinberger and Tucker, the offspring have created the most radical version of the individual in American history—a thoroughly isolated individual who can't make commitments, can't communicate, can't achieve community.

The exclusive emphasis on the self has left many people feeling alone and anxious.

To the extent that organizational offspring remain committed to the self ethic, they are unlikely to provide the human resources for a competitive American work force—not unless the corporation adjusts to them. This is no small problem. There are approximately 19 million adult children of the organization men. What is more, as the offspring of the managerial class, they represent the middle and upper-middle classes—the very people who have historically dominated American business.

The management philosophy of the organization man generation survives. Into the 1990s, corporate managers continue to revere professionalism, control, teamwork, and order. At the same time, they have little patience with the ideas of leadership, substance, or vision. At mid-century, when American companies had no real competition, the organization man's view of corporate reality was viable enough. In the contemporary world of global competition and economic uncertainty, however, vision and leadership may be essential for survival. In the long haul, quality becomes more important than quantity.

Leinberger and Tucker present the grounds for believing that for children of the organization men, the future holds a better fit between their personal style and structural demands. If they are to succeed in the long run, organizations will be required to adapt themselves to a new generation of individualists—men and women who will soon be replacing their fathers in leadership positions. But just in case they don't adapt, perhaps it is time that we study the next generation—the grandchildren of the organization men. ■

■ **FOCUS** *Suggestions for Further Reading*

Concerning "College Fraternities: A Counteracting Force on Campus," the original idea of counteracting forces in mass society can be found in Arnold Rose's article "Reactions Against the Mass Society," in the *Sociological Quarterly* (1962). For a recent treatment of the individual in modern, postmodern, or hypermodern society (depending on your personal view), read the fascinating account by George Ritzer in *The McDonaldization of Society* (1993).

Opposing viewpoints concerning the efficacy of cults are represented in two recent treatments of the topic. On one side, there is the very interesting book *Why Waco? Cults and the Battle for Religious Freedom in America*, in which James Tabor and Eugene Gallagher (1995) present a compelling argument in favor of seeing cult recruits as possessing an active self that can only be manipulated so much. On the other side, Margaret Thaler Singer's (1995) *Cults in Our Midst: The Hidden Menace in Our Everyday Lives* takes the position that cultists are the victims of powerful mind control techniques. For a detailed examination of the details of the Heaven's Gate cult suicide in San Diego, read *Heaven's Gate* by Bill Hoffman and Cathy Burke (1997).

I collected information for "Reunion, American Style" by interviewing alumni personnel in a number of colleges and universities. I also relied on data gathered by the Alumni Administration Division of the Council for the Advancement and Support of Education (CASE). If you are interested in learning more about class reunions, I suggest getting in touch with CASE in Washington, DC. Concerning the functional argument used in this snapshot, Robert K. Merton's *Social Theory and Social Structure* (1957) is an important work in which he discusses, among many other things, the distinction between manifest and latent functions. He also discusses the role of serendipity in science, a topic that will be raised later in this book when we consider social change.

Concerning "Children of the Organization Men," the classic treatment of the midcentury lifestyle of the loyal and obedient corporate employee can be found in William H. Whyte's *The Organization Man* (1956). Conclusions in this snapshot regarding the children of organization men were drawn from *The New Individualists: The Generation After the Organization Man* (1991), by Paul Leinberger and Bruce Tucker. For an enlightening account of how bureaucratic organizations systematically hinder the careers of women, read Rosabeth M. Kanter's *Men and Women of the Corporation* (1993). ■

■ **DEVELOPING IDEAS**  *About the Group Experience*

1. Writing topic: Choose any book which focuses on a dangerous cult (for example, Heaven's Gate, the People's Temple at Jonestown, or David Koresh's Branch Davidians). Based on your reading, write an essay in which you discuss the aspects of the cult which were so influential in making members engage in dangerous behavior. In particular, focus on characteristics of both the leader and followers.

2. Research topic: Do college organizations really compensate for a lack of informal interaction? If so, students who spend much time with family, partners, or friends shouldn't join many clubs and organizations on campus; students who don't hang out with family, partners, or friends should make up the difference by joining. Interview a number of students on your campus to find out as much as you can about their social activities: how often they are with friends or family, how many campus organizations they belong to, any leadership positions they hold in these organizations. What do your results indicate about college organizations as compensatory groups?

3. Writing topic: Examine an institutionalized practice—for example, a wedding or a funeral—for all of the *latent* functions it might perform.

4. Research topic: Just how restrictive is a formal organization? To what extent does holding a job in a large corporation necessitate a loss of personal freedom for the individual who works there? To provide a case study, visit a large company in your local community. For at least a few hours, observe the patterns of behavior including dress, speech, arrangement of furniture in offices, any uniformity of color, hairstyles, cars in the parking lot, schedule for lunch and breaks, and so on. Don't forget to take notes concerning your observations in some systematic way. For example, before beginning, you might want to make a partial list of the patterns of behavior you expect to find, to be expanded during the study. You might even want to visit,

only briefly, another large company, to get ideas about how employees conform. By the way, to avoid looking suspicious while collecting data, you might want to inform someone at the company of your purpose and ask permission to become a participant-observer. ■

# PART FOUR
## Institutions

We can readily see such institutions as a church or senate chamber, but it is more difficult to see how such institutions affect individuals. Whether one functions within the institutions of church or state--as this couple on the left does--or outside of it--as this couple on the right does, they are all products of the institutions in operation in our society.

At a time when today's aging baby boomers were still hippies—during the late 1960s and early 1970s—I was just finishing up my graduate degree and making plans for the future. My primary objective was to teach at the college level. Yet not unlike many of my friends and fellow graduate students in sociology, I also thought long and hard about the possibility of dropping out of the mainstream of competitive American society and establishing instead an alternative lifestyle that would be less demanding and repressive. In retrospect, it sounds kind of silly; but at the time, it seemed to make sense.

During the late 1960s, many young people claimed to have given up on American institutions—the nuclear family, organized religion, capitalism, constitutional government, and traditional forms of public education—and it was relatively easy to find support and encouragement for going it alone. The more politically motivated students of the day referred to anyone in charge of almost anything—whether the police, the chair of the sociology department, or the president of the United States—as "pigs" and to conventional, middle-class political institutions, in the most negative sense possible, as "the establishment." Even among students who weren't inclined toward politics, the operating principle of everyday life seemed to be "do your own thing." Traditional institutions—the traditional ways of meeting basic needs—were often viewed as irrelevant, if not the enemy.

Of course, though many hip-oriented students paid lip service to the idea of an alternative lifestyle, most never went much beyond the hippie fashion (wearing love beads, jeans, and long hair) in seeking to throw off what they saw as the yoke of repression represented by American institutions. Even the antiwar demonstrations and demonstrations for civil rights and women were, for the most part, designed to reform, not overthrow, traditional institutional arrangements. After all, many of those young people who demonstrated loudly for equal rights or against the war were students enrolled in the very colleges and universities they were fiercely attacking. Moreover, only a relatively few young people actually left school to drop out of American society.

Over time, those who did leave to take up residence on a commune attempted to establish their own institutions—frequently, collective arrangements for feeding their families, building shelter, making clothing, teaching the basic skills of everyday life to children, and attending to their spiritual needs. Many communes failed to survive for more than a few months, however, because they also failed to develop collective ways for meeting their members' basic needs. In a word, they never developed viable alternative institutions.

The collective ways developed by any society for meeting the economic, religious, familial, political, and educational needs of its members are known as *institutions*. The lesson to be learned from the failure of many hippie communes of the 1960s and 1970s is simply that a group of people cannot survive very long as a group without generating some set of effective institutional arrangements. The more recent demise of the Soviet Union was, in part, a result of a profound failure of its institutions in terms of meeting the basic needs of its members. It can happen to a small commune or to an entire society of millions of people.

How well do American institutions meet human needs? In "Who's Minding the Kids?" we find a very negative answer: Our families, schools, and religious institutions are so weak that the adolescent peer group has taken over. Young people now raise one another. As a result, violence among teenagers has taken on epidemic proportions.

Institutions often provide an efficiency in meeting human needs that would be impossible by sheer individual effort alone. But on the social psychological level, institutional responsiveness to difficult social problems also allows human beings to avoid dealing firsthand with what they desire to pretend doesn't exist—death, illness, disaster, disfigurement, and disability.

In "Let the System Do It!" this idea is introduced and illustrated. We have developed a set of institutions—schools, political systems, corporations, legal units, and religions—each of which now carries out specialized functions that used to be performed by family members. As a result, we, as individual members of society, escape the burden of having to face the entire range of human issues and frailties.

Another negative aspect of our institutions is contained in "Americans Are Moving to the Margins of Society." It isn't only government that has suffered recently with respect to loss of credibility; there is much evidence to suggest that faith and confidence in all mainstream institutions are on the decline.

One of the most important functions of the economic institution involves getting the unpleasant but necessary jobs done. In "Dirty Work," we are reminded that dirty work in America has traditionally been performed at low wages by poor people, newcomers, and minorities who have had few other choices. We also see that the "dirtiness" of a job has little, if anything, to do with its being physically unclean but can be changed profoundly depending on how much we pay people to do it. ■

# Who's Minding the Kids?
## Is Violence Filling the Void in Our Teenagers' Lives?

Daily, the headlines scream of hideous crimes—drive-by shootings, carjackings, and senseless murders—committed by our nation's teenagers. What makes violence so appealing to so many youngsters? Why is it that, in many quarters around the country, guns have replaced leather jackets and CD players as status symbols of choice?

According to police reports to the FBI, the number of homicides committed by youngsters in their early teens has recently skyrocketed. Between 1985 and 1991, arrest rates for homicide increased among 13- and 14-year-old males by 140%; among 15-year-old males by 217%.

Actually, the problem has been even worse than these dreadful statistics might suggest. While relatively few of our youngsters are committing hideous murders, they are being tolerated—perhaps even honored—by their friends and classmates. Millions of teenagers may not be able to shoot or stab someone themselves, but they are fully capable of looking on as others do so.

Several years ago, a case of bystander apathy raised enough concern to inspire the movie *River's Edge*. A teenager in Milpitas, California murdered his 14-year-old girlfriend and then returned to the scene with a dozen classmates to show them the corpse. One student covered the body with leaves to keep it from being discovered; others threw rocks at it. None of them contacted the police or told their parents.

More recently, the nation was shocked to learn that an attractive New Hampshire school teacher, Pam Smart, had inspired her 15-year-old student and his friends to eliminate her husband, Greg, by shooting him in the head. Attorney Marsha Kazarosian subsequently filed a suit against the Winnecunnet, New Hampshire school district on behalf of the families of the three youngsters convicted in the murder. Kazarosian claimed that Pam Smart's love affair with her student was made possible because she was negligently unsupervised by the Winnecunnet High School administration—that somebody in charge should have been keeping a watchful eye on Smart.

Whether or not school officials should have known, it appears that they may have been the only ones at Winnecunnet High who didn't.

Statements made during the course of the police investigation indicate clearly that at least 1 month before the police finally broke the case, the corridors of Winnecunnet High were already abuzz with rumors implicating the three students and their teacher. Yet nobody bothered to inform an adult.

More incredibly, statements later made to law enforcement officials indicate that students at Winnecunnet High were talking about Greg Smart's murder for 2 months *before* it actually occurred. With a simple phone call, any one of them might have prevented a murder. But nobody wanted to "snitch" or "tattle" on a classmate. Everybody was concerned about being rejected by friends. So they all kept quiet and let the murder plot proceed according to plan.

Too many of our teenagers have become desensitized to the consequences of violence. They have been raised on a steady diet of slasher films filled with gory scenes of sex, murder, and mayhem. After school, they come home to an empty house, where they spend hours daily listening to rap and heavy metal lyrics or watching MTV videos in which violence is glorified. For economic reasons, more and more of our teenagers are left to fend for themselves, unsupervised after school and during vacations.

Only a few of our youngsters are willing to shoot someone in the head. But many others participate from a distance. Even if breaking their silence might stop a murder, they do not want to get involved.

It may have happened in New Hampshire, but it could have been anywhere. Marsha Kazarosian's lawsuit reflects an unpleasant truth about American society today. It isn't that TV, motion pictures, and popular music are so powerful. It is that our traditional institutions have become so weak. Our schools, religions, and families have lost their moral authority. And in their place, we have allowed the peer group to fill the void in our youngsters' lives. ∎

# Let the System Do It!
## Taking Care of Society's Problems Can Hurt

Less than a century ago, the middle-class family was still involved in almost every aspect of its members' lives. Mother, father, grandparents, and children all worked the farm (or in the family firm). Together, they educated the offspring, treated illnesses, and provided a role for elders. After death, family members were buried in the family plot in the backyard, not in some cemetery with thousands of strangers located miles away.

In responding to social problems, we have similarly constructed hospitals, prisons, nursing homes, and "special" schools for the retarded and the emotionally disturbed. In the same way, we have built mental institutions, cancer wards, soup kitchens, and retirement communities—all in the name of efficiency and humanitarian motivation.

Clearly, there are compelling administrative, medical, and economic reasons why many of our thorniest human problems—illness, poverty, and old age—are better handled by specialized formal organizations than by families. But there may be other, less rational, reasons as well.

One clue is to look at the sites where our nation's prisons and mental hospitals were first located. Many of them are now in middle-class suburban areas, an easy drive from the urban core. But at the time they were built, these same areas were quite different—they were almost invariably secluded rural settings, located many miles from large population centers and hidden from everyday view. Even cemeteries were typically built some distance from major cities, allowing friends and relatives to pay a visit but only on a limited basis.

Remember the cliche "out of sight, out of mind"? Let's face it: There are many problems that middle-class Americans would prefer to shuttle aside and put out of easy reach. Too often, the attitude is, "Let somebody else take care of it. We aren't trained and they are."

Thus, our formal organizations help us to isolate those things we simply don't want to see. By constructing a formal response, we are able to avoid the whole range of human misery that might otherwise disrupt our personal lives and make us feel very uncomfortable. By letting the formal system take care of terminal cancer patients, drug addicts, severely disfigured individuals, and Alzheimer's victims, for example, we increase the *subjective probability* that these hideous things won't happen to us or to our loved ones. By distancing ourselves from human frailty and misery, we are then free to pursue our individual goals and objectives—at work and at home—without fear that *the same thing might (or will) happen to us.*

Specialized institutions give us the false security of being able to go through life avoiding life's problems—until we are forced to deal with them. This may be one reason why community-based forms of treatment for mental illness, retardation, and juvenile delinquency have so often been opposed by Americans. In too many cases, even where their residents pose little if any risk to the neighbors, the thinking is that halfway houses belong on anybody else's block but mine.

Of course, not everyone opts to put their blinders on. Recognizing the myopic view of many Americans, educators are beginning to stress the importance of exposing young people to the entire range of social problems that they might otherwise not encounter. In one special program for high school students, for example, each teenager in the program spends one day working in a home for retarded children, each spends a number of hours in a jail cell, and each pays a visit to a morgue. They may get sick to their stomachs, but they also learn about the possible consequences of their own behavior as well as the inevitable consequences of being human. They are forced to see the world the way it really is and not the way they'd like it to be. In the process, they may unexpectedly come face-to-face with themselves. ■

# Americans Are Moving to the Margins of Society
They No Longer Trust Mainstream Solutions

What does the Oklahoma City massacre have in common with the mass suicide of 39 Heaven's Gate cultists near San Diego? Both of these tragedies provide additional examples of Americans who are turning, in ever increasing numbers, to the margins of society—rather than to its mainstream—for solutions to their personal problems. Twenty or thirty years ago, citizens searching for spiritual guidance would, in all likelihood, have received comfort and reassurance from their church and family; those seeking a political answer would have found it in the Democratic or Republican party. Now they are more likely to join an obscure cult, go into the woods on Sunday afternoons to rehearse for the coming apocalypse, or simply barricade themselves in their homes rather than obey a federal court order.

All of our traditional institutions are under attack. Postmodernists turn their backs on the scientific method, claiming that it has helped to destroy civilization; skeptical patients experiment with herbal or homeopathic medicine, megavitamin therapy, acupuncture, or Tai Chi; and increasing numbers of parents have given up on the public schools, opting for a private-school alternative or for educating their youngsters at home.

Their credibility with the American people having plummeted to new depths, our leaders now have the stature of stereotypical used car salesmen. In a recent Gallup survey, only 9% of all adult Americans voiced a great deal of confidence in the executive branch of government, only 10% in Congress. Three quarters of Americans are convinced that the government is somehow involved in conspiracies, and two in five Americans continue to believe it has covered up information about the TWA 800 jet disaster in 1996. Pierre Salinger is far from the Lone Ranger when it comes to being suspicious of the FBI or the CIA.

Outside of government, moreover, our institutions are faring only slightly better. When asked to evaluate the honesty and ethical standards of various occupational groups, less than 20% of the American people gave very high marks to labor union leaders, real estate agents, lawyers, stockbrokers, business executives, newspaper reporters, TV commentators, bankers, police, dentists, medical doctors, college teachers, or even clergy.

Part of the reason for the erosion of trust and confidence in traditional institutions involves the eclipse of community we have recently experienced. Many Americans feel they have no place to turn when they get into trouble—they are unable to find a sense of belonging and importance at work, among friends, or in their own families. Children come home from school to an empty house. Anxious not to be fired or laid off, their parents are too busy at work to get to know their neighbors or participate in community activities. Those who have moved their residence for the sake of a job no longer have friends, family, or fraternal organizations to help them through tough times. Their support systems are now hundreds, perhaps thousands, of miles away. Even if they have remained in the same community, growing numbers of families are without the assistance of extended kin, especially grandparents, or of two parents who can share the tasks of child rearing and family breadwinning. As income inequality continues to rise, the eclipse of community becomes increasingly burdensome.

The decline in institutional credibility also involves a 30-year spiral of scandals involving leadership at the highest levels of government, business, and entertainment—Chappaquiddick, Abscam, Irangate, Watergate, S&L, Travelgate, Filegate, and the recent campaign financing fiasco—not to mention the assumed and actual transgressions committed by Robert Packwood, Newt Gingrich, Bill Clinton, Michael Milken, Leona Helmsley, and Michael Jackson.

As we approach the year 2000, growing numbers of Americans are thinking in apocalyptic terms. Some expect a spiritual transition to a higher plane, while others believe that the new millennium will bring the ultimate physical confrontation and destruction in a war of all against all.

We cannot do anything to alter the calendar—hopefully, our nation will survive to new heights in the next millennium. As individuals, we are almost as powerless to influence the course of our economy at the federal level. But all of us can assume a special sense of responsibility for what happens in our own backyard—at work, in our neighborhoods and schools, and at home. It is at the grassroots level that we might begin to repair the credibility of our traditional institutions. This is where we can make an effort on behalf of our fellow citizens in trouble so that they feel important, special, a sense of belonging, that they really count. Bringing Americans back into the mainstream may be our only realistic chance to prevent more mass suicides and acts of domestic terrorism in the future. ∎

# Dirty Work
## Who's Going to Do the Unpleasant Jobs?

Every society has its "dirty work": jobs that are considered repugnant, undignified, or menial. They may also be regarded as absolutely essential for the well-being of society. Throughout the world, much of the dirtiest work of a society has been reserved for those individuals considered to be outside the mainstream; for example, Pakistanis in England, Iraqis in Kuwait, and Turks in Germany. At the same time, even the most prestigious occupations may include at least a few tasks that could be regarded as dirty.

As a historical trend, the increasing rationalization of American society has created a proliferation of specialized occupations from what was formerly thought of as merely another field's dirty work. Indeed, millions of Americans currently work in jobs that never even existed a few decades earlier: assistants to activity directors in nursing homes and day care centers, emergency medical technicians, dental hygienists, data entry personnel, paralegals, associate producers, home care workers, audiovisual equipment aides, television and radio interns, and so on. To an increasing extent, therefore, one occupation's dirty work has become another's raison d'être!

In the midst of the expansion of specialized occupational roles, some professionals have gained enough resources to subcontract much, if not all, of their dirty work to lower-paid specialists. For example, professors may assign the task of grading multiple-choice exams to their teaching assistants, many dentists have hygienists who perform routine dental care, and nurses often enlist nurses' aides to change bandages and bedpans. Accountants have their bookkeepers, physicians have physicians' assistants, and lawyers have paralegals.

What comes to be viewed as dirty work need not be the least bit dirty, at least in a physical sense. There is really nothing intrinsically repulsive about what we might choose to call dirty work. Instead, jobs are labeled as respectable or dirty based typically on a social construction: The members of a society share an understanding of the nature of their environment and apply that understanding to their definitions of occupational tasks.

In contemporary American society, for example, bankers are generally seen as holding a reputable occupational position. During the Middle Ages, however, the same job was regarded as too dirty for Christians to perform and was instead assigned to outsiders—specifically, to European Jews who were systematically excluded from respectable activities such as farming, owning land, and joining the guilds of craftsmen. Generally, Jews were restricted to the despised occupation of lending money at interest—an activity regarded as essential by the church and the nobility as a source of outside financing for building, farming, waging war, or engaging in political affairs.

Its economic importance notwithstanding, usury was absolutely forbidden to the Christian majority on religious grounds. As viewed by the church, the lending of money for interest was sinful regardless of the amount of interest charged or the purpose for which money was borrowed. Thus, any Christian who lent money during the Middle Ages would have committed a mortal sin. In the view of the medieval church, however, Jews were headed for hell anyway, so their participation in money lending could add little to the eternal punishment that already awaited them in the hereafter.

Traditionally, dirty work in America has been performed at low wages by poor people, newcomers, and minorities who have had few other choices. In the southern colonies, slaves were forced to play the role of field hands or domestic servants, and indentured servants performed heavy labor to buy their freedom. During the 19th century, Chinese newcomers toiled to build the railroads and work the crops. At the turn of the 20th century, European immigrants performed unskilled, backbreaking labor for poor wages and under miserable working conditions.

Even today, many economic activities involving dirty work in areas such as restaurants, hospitals, and industrial agriculture continue to rely heavily on people from outside the mainstream—Americans of color and newcomers from Latin America, Asia, and Eastern Europe. According to sociologist Herbert Gans, these activities could not survive in their present form without depending on the substandard wages that they pay to their employees. More generally, Gans suggests that poverty may actually persist in part because it serves the important function of providing a low-wage labor pool that is willing to perform dirty work at low cost.

Of course, many respectable jobs also involve at least some tasks that most people would consider boring and unpleasant, even if they don't require getting their hands dirty. Take, for example, the role of police officer, which, according to the television image, consists exclusively of battling the forces of evil. Actually, the police spend much of their time and energy on more mundane matters, such as removing dead mice, controlling traffic, doing paperwork, helping citizens who have fallen out of bed, and answering false alarms. Many police officers actually go through an entire career without ever having to fire their weapons in the line of duty.

To complicate matters, the very meaning of what comes to be regarded as dirty work is partially determined by the prestige level of an occupation. Indeed, the same tasks may be considered dirty when performed for low wages but respectable and clean when performed for a lot of money. Homemakers who are unpaid for providing services to the members of their family may occasionally feel bored with routine child rearing and the daily drudgery of preparing the evening meal, yet such tasks are not intrinsically boring. In fact, they are quite pleasant and satisfying—when carried out by a well-paid teacher or by a chef in a gourmet restaurant. One can only wonder what might happen to the desirability ratings of cooking and child rearing if homemakers were paid a decent daily wage.

Many people are physically sickened by the image of doctors as they perform surgery on their patients or, worse yet, conduct an autopsy. More than a few neophyte medical students have been known to go rubbery at the sight of a cadaver being anatomized. Yet Americans would hardly identify the role of doctor with dirty work. Instead, physicians continue to enjoy extremely high status with the American public, invariably being ranked ahead of most other occupations with respect to prestige. Apparently, even the most repulsive job is not necessarily thought of as dirty work. Is it a doctor's life-and-death struggle that makes the difference? In part, perhaps. But high income, prestige, and power can usually be counted on to turn the dirtiest work into good, clean fun! ∎

■ **FOCUS** *Suggestions for Further Reading*

In "Who's Minding the Kids?" I suggest that the peer group has filled a void left by the absence of other strong institutions. To see the long-term trend in the rise of the peer group in relation to changes in the family, I recommend David Riesman's *The Lonely Crowd* (1950). Even with the passage of decades, this classic work continues to teach us about American social character. Riesman sees the major source of socialization as having changed, with larger shifts in social character from tradition-directed to inner-directed to other-directed types. Until the mid-20th century, parents continued to be the primary agents of socialization for youngsters. Children internalized a set of normative criteria during their early years that remained with them for life to guide their behavior. More recently, however, parents were replaced by the peer group as the major source of values and norms. Many youngsters became motivated not to please their parents but to gain the approval of their friends, associates, or contemporaries. They acted not so much out of an internal sense of what was right and wrong but more out of a desire to do what the peer group believed to be right and wrong.

"Let the System Do It!" focuses attention on the rise of specialized institutions that, for the sake of efficiency, may have reduced the psychological burden of death and illness in our daily lives. German sociologist Max Weber long ago discussed this trend in modern society when he wrote about "rationalization"—the process whereby our lives have become increasingly dominated by institutions dedicated to efficiency and to the domination of human beings by technology. Weber recognized that we pay a price for this efficiency: the dehumanization of everyday life. For a discussion of Weber's treatment of rationalization, see Stephen Kalberg's "Max Weber's Types of Rationality: Cornerstones for the Analysis of *Rationalization* Processes in History," in the *American Journal of Sociology* (1980). Two excellent recent books by George Ritzer analyze modern life using Weber's concept of rationalization: *The McDonaldization of Society* (1993), about the fast-food industry, and *Expressing America* (1995), about our use of credit cards.

In "Americans Are Moving to the Margins of Society," I contend that the credibility of all conventional institutions has recently slipped. To see for yourself, in comparative terms, just how far institutional confidence has fallen over the decades, page through the latest version (it comes out annually) of the Bureau of Justice Statistics' *Sourcebook of Criminal Justice Statistics*. Look in the index for the section on "attitudes."

Concerning "Dirty Work," I drew much of my discussion from an earlier project with Bill Levin, *The Functions of Discrimination and Prejudice* (1982). Sociologist Everett Hughes investigates a particularly hideous form of dirty work in an article in *Social Problems* titled "Good People and Dirty Work" (1962). In this article, Hughes attempted to come to grips with the factors that led otherwise ordinary Germans to work in concentration camps during the Nazi regime. Dirty work as part of the division of labor in a society, what Émile Durkheim calls "organic solidarity," can be seen in Durkheim's classic book *The Division of Labor in Society*, which he wrote in 1933. A specific, if unexpected, form of dirty work is covered by Teresa Gowen (1998). In her study of "American untouchables," she locates the importance of homeless trash recyclers in the larger recycling efforts of the city of San Francisco. ∎

■ **DEVELOPING IDEAS** *About Institutions*

1. Writing topic: Imagine that all institutions suddenly ceased to exist and that you personally had no choice but to take care of satisfying your own needs (and the needs of family members) on a daily basis. Write a short essay in which you describe a typical day in your life.

2. Writing topic: As indicated earlier, *The Sourcebook of Criminal Justice Statistics,* published yearly by the Department of Justice, is a gold mine of data concerning Americans' attitudes toward conventional institutions. Using the information in the *Sourcebook* as a basis, construct a number of tables showing how Americans have changed their opinion of the criminal justice system—police, courts, prisons, judges, and so on—since the 1970s.

3. Research topic: What is a family and what is not? To study the range of family conceptions held by college students, construct a short questionnaire and give it to a small sample of students on your campus. One approach would be for you to give your respondents a list of possible family arrangements that you develop beforehand and then ask them to evaluate each of the arrangements as a legitimate family form. For example, you might include (a) mother, father, and children; (b) mother and children; (c) father and children; (d) mother, boyfriend, and children; (e) father, girlfriend, and children; (f) gay couple and children; (g) mother, stepfather, and children; (h) woman living alone; (i) college roommates; (j) grandparents and grandchildren; and so on.

4. Writing topic: In a short essay, discuss changes in the structure and functions of the family over the last 30 years. If you have completed the research topic above, how do you think your respondents would have answered the same question about family, if you had asked them 30 years ago?

5. Research topic: Traditionally, garbage collecting has been viewed as dirty work, not only because it was physically unclean but also because it was a low-paying job. Collecting garbage is still physically dirty, but is it still low paying? To see how the dirtiness of garbage collecting may have changed over the years, compare the average income of garbage collectors in your town or state, or nationally, now versus 10, 20, and 30 years ago. Also determine whether the collectors are unionized

and how often they have threatened to strike. If it is possible and makes sense, compare the racial or ethnic composition of garbage collectors over time. Why might you expect a change in race or ethnic group? As a final possibility, examine in detail the circumstances of any strike that might have occurred among garbage collectors in your town. How long did it last? Just how much were garbage pickups missed during the strike? Did the strike disrupt business or school? How was the strike resolved? ∎

# PART FIVE

## Deviance

What's bad, wrong, illegal, and immoral? An act of deviance, of course! Usually we think of criminals as deviants, but as these essays show, those with interests contrary to the society's norms are treated with ridicule and scorn. Being fat in our society is like being dealt a prison sentence--society assumes something bad about the obese and indicts them as guilty of a sin or crime, when in reality, they have committed neither.

The last time I visited a state prison, it was to interview a notorious serial killer. As you might expect, our conversation began in a rather tentative manner. I tried to figure out what he was thinking; he tried to figure out what I was up to. I sized him up; he sized me up. Our first 30 minutes together consisted of an exchange of polite trivialities. We talked about most everything—everything, that is, except what I had come to discuss in the first place: the heinous crimes for which he had been convicted.

If you've ever visited a prison, you probably know how uncomfortable it can be to talk with inmates, at least initially. There is usually a great deal of anxiety, and it gets in the way of honest communication.

Part of the problem involves what sociologist Erving Goffman referred to as "the management of spoiled identity." An imprisoned serial murderer has been stigmatized; he is totally discredited among those who live beyond the prison walls. He knows that I know, and I know that he knows that I know. There is no way for him to conceal the fact that he has been found guilty of murdering 12 young women, even if he continues to proclaim his innocence (which serial killers almost always do). The prison walls tell it all. So the best we can expect to do is to minimize the discomfort generated by his deviance—and that takes both time and effort.

*Deviance* refers to any behavior of an individual that violates the norms and values of a group or society generally. Many acts of deviance are rather harmless; for example, parking in a loading zone or breaking a curfew. Other acts of deviance are incredibly dangerous and violent. When someone commits a severely deviant act, he or she may be stigmatized. In other words, the violation of society's rules is regarded as so extreme that an entire human being, and not just a particular behavior, gets discredited. Clearly, serial killers fit this category. But as suggested in "Fat Chance in a Slim World," so do individuals who are overweight by conventional standards—and they haven't broken any laws at all! Fat is too often regarded as a symptom of not just illness but also a lack of moral fiber or willpower. To some extent, people who are "too" short, tall, or thin also bear the burden.

Mentally ill patients represent another group of stigmatized people. Some very depressed individuals would rather conceal their pain and suffering than risk being rejected by the important people in their lives. As suggested in "You Must Get Ill First; Then

You Recover," those mental patients who are hospitalized also risk labeling. According to Erving Goffman, they may be thoroughly resocialized so that they can be easily managed and controlled. Goffman contends that new patients learn quickly what is required of them to get along while institutionalized and, later, to be released. Rosenhan's experiment in the same essay indicates clearly what happens when mental patients refuse to cooperate—they continue to be regarded as sick.

French sociologist Émile Durkheim once observed that deviant behavior actually helps to unite the members of a society by focusing attention on the validity of its moral order. In the face of a deviant act—for example, a heinous crime—the members of a group feel challenged, even threatened. They no longer take for granted the important values that they share. Instead, they rally their forces to encourage and support the legitimacy of "behaving correctly." Durkheim also suggested that punishing the individual who commits a deviant act similarly reconfirms behavior that conforms to a group's cultural standards. Punishment sends a message to every member of society: "Listen, buddy. Break the rules and the same thing will happen to you!"

Numerous Americans, concerned about our soaring crime rate, would gladly base their support of capital punishment on Durkheim's view of deviance: Sending a killer to the electric chair also sends a message to potential killers everywhere. Thus, capital punishment is often justified by the fact that it might serve as a *deterrent* to violent crime. As indicated in "Is the Death Penalty Only a Vehicle for Revenge?" however, there is very little evidence to suggest that capital punishment actually deters future murderers (although it definitely deters the condemned killer from killing again). Even if most Americans favor capital punishment, most criminologists seem to agree that the *swift* and *certain* imposition of a life sentence without parole is an effective alternative to the death penalty. First-degree murderers should never be eligible for parole or furlough, and their sentences should never be commuted by a future governor who believes in their rehabilitation. As criminologist James A. Fox and I have argued, "We need a 'life sentence without hope.'"

Let me pause, at this point, to once again raise the question of "value-free" sociology. In "Is the Death Penalty Only a Vehicle for Revenge?" I take a definite stand—based on evidence collected by criminologists, but nevertheless a definite stand—on a controversial issue. You should be aware that some sociologists would cringe at the very thought. In their view, the advocacy role is antithetical to the goals of the "science of sociology." Not everyone would agree, however. Sociologist Howard Becker has in fact argued just the opposite: that sociologists must take sides in favor of important values and pressing concerns. For him, the advocacy role is not only consistent with but essential to the work of sociology.

I am especially sure that the death penalty would have little impact on mass murderers. Those who kill several victims at a time would hardly be deterred by either a life sentence or an execution. Indeed, their killing spree is usually an act of suicide anyway, but before taking their own life, they have decided to get even with all of those individuals they blame for having caused their problems—*all* women, *all* foreigners, *all* postal workers, and so on.

Historically, the death penalty has been discriminatory in its application. For crimes of equivalent severity, black defendants were more likely than their white counterparts to be executed by the state. In 1972, the Supreme Court declared the death penalty unconstitutional because it was being applied in an uneven, capricious manner. In 1976, it was reinstated but only if applied under strict guidelines. Even today, there is evidence that the administration of the death penalty is uneven. Offenders who kill white victims "get the chair" more often than those offenders who kill black victims. Since 1976, on a national level, 65 blacks have been executed for murdering white victims, but only one white person has been executed for the death of a black victim.

One of the more challenging yet important tasks of sociology is to be able to predict deviant behavior; for example, who will turn out to be a hardened criminal and who won't. While we are still far from being able to make such predictions, a recent study which I co-authored with Arnold Arluke suggests that animal abuse may be a warning sign for violence committed against humans. In fact, our study indicates that cruelty toward animals may be linked with all forms of antisocial behavior, both violent and nonviolent. Of course, this clearly does not mean that every child who intentionally harms a dog or a cat will grow up to be a hardened criminal. Indeed, most will not. This leaves us in the uncomfortable position of understanding an important factor *symptomatic of* many forms of deviant behavior but of being unable to predict future behavior. The problem is one of false positives—many abusers grow up and out of their deviant behavior.

Of course, some youngsters don't wait to grow up before they exhibit criminal behavior. This was made painfully clear as investigators around the country—and especially in southern states—attempted to solve the hundreds of cases of arson being targeted at America's churches. It very quickly become obvious that black churches were being disproportionately victimized, though many white churches had been burned as well. The over-representation of black churches gave some legitimacy to the opinion that many of the burnings were racially inspired. As it turned out, however, most of the burnings of black churches could not be pinned on any conspiracy on the part of organized hate groups. Sadly, most of the assailants represented America's future—its children. ∎

# Fat Chance in a Slim World
We Believe It's the Size of a Book's Cover That Counts

A black woman in Philadelphia recently wrote complaining about the way she was treated by other people. Among other things, she rarely dated, had few friends, and was forced to settle for a job for which she was overqualified. Moreover, passengers on buses and trains often stared at her with pity or scorn, while workers at the office rarely included her in their watercooler conversations.

The letter writer attributed these difficulties not to her gender or race but to the fact that she was vastly overweight by conventional standards. Her letter brought to mind the unfortunate victims of illnesses such as cancer, heart disease, and Alzheimer's disease who have the unavoidable symptoms of an illness over which they have little, if any, control. But they are typically treated with compassion and sympathy.

Curiously enough, fat people frequently receive contempt rather than compassion, unless their obesity can be attributed to some physical ailment (e.g., a "glandular condition"). Otherwise, they are seen as having caused their own problem by some combination of excessive impulsivity and lack of moral fiber. Not unlike prostitutes, ex-cons and homeless people, they may be regarded as lacking in the self-control and willpower necessary to lead a healthy, normal life. In addition, this discrimination has been directed more often at women than at men over the years.

The term *fat person* is therefore more than a description of somebody's weight, body type, or illness; more often than not, it is also used to stigmatize or discredit an entire group of human beings by making their belt size an excuse for bigotry. The lady from Philadelphia may have been correct: Research suggests that people who are overweight by our standards are often viewed as undesirable dates and mates. They frequently have trouble getting married, going to college, obtaining credit from a bank, or being promoted. In short, they are excluded, exploited, and oppressed.

Stigmatizing fat people is, of course, only one expression of a much more general tendency in our culture: the tendency to judge others by their looks rather than their intelligence, talent, or character. Study after study suggests that "what is beautiful is good!" That is, attractive individuals are more likely to be preferred as dates, to be popular with their friends, to be cuddled and kissed as newborns, to achieve high grades in school, to be disciplined less severely by their parents, to be recommended for a job after a personal interview, and to have their written work judged favorably.

By conventional American wisdom, fat is as ugly and deviant as thin is beautiful. We are so infatuated with being slim and trim that it is indeed hard to imagine anything else. Yet the desirability of particular body types and body weight varies from culture to culture. Beginning with the ancient world, fat has not always been universally despised. Instead, fat people were often respected, if not admired, throughout history. Even Cleopatra was fat by our standards, although by the standards of her own time and culture, she was a raving beauty. Renoir's French impressionist masterpieces similarly portrayed a version of the female body that today would be considered massive, huge, and fat rather than beautiful. And in cultures where food was in short supply, obesity was often used to validate personal success. Under such circumstances, rich people could afford to eat enough to be fat and therefore to survive. Skinny was therefore a sign of neither good health nor beauty but a symptom of poverty and illness.

Until the Roaring Twenties, the large and voluptuous version of feminine beauty continued to dominate in our culture. But the flappers changed all this by bobbing their hair, binding their breasts and, by some accounts, trying to resemble "adolescent boys." While many women of the 1920s moved toward feminine power, others retreated from it by shrinking their bodies in fad diets. The result was that during this era, the suffragist movement succeeded and women got the vote, but many men felt threatened. All of a sudden, they preferred women who were small, petite, and thin, who looked powerless.

Given the importance of physical attractiveness in defining the value and achievement of females, it should come as no surprise that American women have come under extreme pressure to be unrealistically slim and trim. This may have made many women dissatisfied with their bodies and mistakenly convinced them that mastery was possible only by controlling their weight. Women constitute 90% of those afflicted with the eating disorder anorexia nervosa and are the majority of those who join organizations such as Weight Watchers and Diet Workshop. Women are also more likely than men to suffer from compulsive overeating and obesity.

Since the women's movement of the 1960s, we seem to have become even more preoccupied with being slim and trim. *Playboy's* centerfolds and contestants in the Miss America pageant have become increasingly thin. Leading women's magazines publish more and more articles about diets and dieting. Physicians offer drastic medical "cures," such as stomach stapling for obesity and liposuction surgery for "problem areas" like "saddlebag" thighs, "protuberant" abdomens, buttocks, "love handles," fatty knees, and redundant chins. And the best-seller list inevitably contains a disproportionate number of books promising miraculous methods of weight reduction.

In the face of all this, signs of an incipient cultural rebellion against crash dieting and irrational thinness have emerged. Popular books such as Millman's *Such a Pretty Face*, Orbach's *Fat Is a Feminist Issue*, and Chernin's *The Obsession: Reflections on the Tyranny of Slenderness* have taken their place in bookstores alongside the diet manuals. But rather than urge obedience to the conventional standards of beauty, these new books expose the dangers to physical and mental health due to rapid and repeated weight loss. Rather than focus on individual change, they place the blame for our excessive concern with being skinny on sexism and the socialization of women to absurd cultural standards.

The merchants of fashion have also sensed a cultural change in the offing. Growing numbers of dress shops now specialize in "designer fashions for size 14 and over" and "flattering designs in better plus size fashions." Moreover, based on a good deal of evidence from around the world, physicians have revised their weight standards so that what was formerly considered 10 or 15 pounds overweight is now regarded as optimal.

As a final element in this dynamic, organizations such as the National Association to Aid Fat Americans (NAAFA) have helped fat people—even those who are considered obese—to gain a more favorable self-image. Rather than automatically advising its members to diet, NAAFA calls attention to the fact that fat people are often the victims of prejudice and discrimination. It recognizes the dangers in rapid and repeated weight loss and focuses instead on improving the way that fat people are treated on the job, as customers, and in social situations. Taking its cue from black organizations, which reject words originating in the white community such as *Negro* and *colored*, NAAFA prefers to use the term *fat* rather than *overweight* or *obese*. In this way, it refuses to conceal the issue in euphemisms, refuses to accept the stigma, and emphasizes that "fat can be beautiful!"

Unfortunately, however, our culture continues to give fat people a double message. On the one hand, we advise them to be themselves and to accept their body image regardless of social pressures to conform to some arbitrary standard of beauty. On the other hand, we urge them to go on a diet so that they will no longer be deviant. While the rhetoric may be confusing, it is also revealing. All things considered, our aversion is deeply embedded in our culture and is likely to remain with us for some time to come. ∎

# You Must Get Ill First; Then You Recover
## Checking Out of a Mental Hospital May Be Harder Than Checking In

Sociologist Erving Goffman's study of the way patients were treated in a mental hospital yielded some frightening conclusions. He found that the hospital staff assumed absolute power to define how patients should think and behave. The institution gained total control over the terms by which its patients defined themselves. Inmates were thoroughly resocialized so that they could be easily managed and controlled.

According to Goffman, new patients learned quickly what was required of them to get along while institutionalized and, later, to be released. They were asked to discard their old self-concepts—those they had used "on the outside"—and to adopt a new set of self-definitions taught by the staff. First and foremost, inmates were to abandon the normal concept that they were "sane" or "healthy" and instead see themselves as "sick" and therefore in need of help. Admitting that they were psychologically ill was regarded as a patient's first step along "the road to recovery." Conversely, any claim that an inmate was "well" was regarded as a symptom of severe mental disease.

As patients spent more and more time in the hospital, larger areas of their self-concept were "turned upside down." Boredom was regarded as a sign of depression, anger as "acting out," independence as rebelliousness and irrationality, and a desire for privacy as withdrawal. It took no time at all for inmates to recognize that being resocialized by the institution to accept the role of a mentally ill person was the only way to be rewarded while confined and then later to be regarded as cured. This meant not being a management problem for the staff—submitting to the hospital routines, which included cooperation in taking medications and going to therapy sessions. Otherwise, a patient might remain in the institution indefinitely.

Ideally, of course, whether a patient is defined by the hospital staff as healthy or sick and viewed as ready for release should be based strictly on his or her symptoms. In reality, however, the social setting of a mental hospital also comes into play in defining the situation.

This brings up an interesting question that sounds very much like the plot from an old movie: If perfectly normal and healthy people were secretly admitted to a mental hospital, would they be able to convince the staff that they were well, that they didn't belong, that they should be released? Or would they be defined by the rules of hospital life as rebellious, irrational, depressed, and therefore in need of continuing hospitalization?

A classic study by D. L. Rosenhan looked at exactly this question. He had eight sane individuals—five men and three women representing a range of ages and occupations—secretly admitted to one of a number of mental hospitals across the country. Each of Rosenhan's "pseudopatients" was totally free of any symptoms of mental illness; all of them gained admission by complaining that they "had been hearing voices." No hospital staff members were informed about the study.

Based only on this one symptom, hearing voices, all but one of the pseudopatients were diagnosed as suffering from schizophrenia. Moreover, once inside the hospital, the pseudopatients stopped expressing any symptoms of illness. They spoke and behaved normally for the entire duration of their stay.

When the pseudopatients expressed their desire to be discharged, they were told that release depended on the ability of a patient to convince the staff that he or she was sane. Yet despite their normal behavior, the average length of hospitalization for the group was 19 days. One of them failed to be released for 52 days. Finally, all of the pseudopatients were discharged—but with a diagnosis of "schizophrenia in remission." In other words, not one was able to convince a hospital staff of his or her sanity, only that the symptoms of his or her illness had subsided.

In case you were wondering whether *anyone,* staff or not, would have been fooled by Rosenhan's band of pseudopatients, we have an answer for you. Believe it or not, some 25% of the other patients on the admissions wards accused the pseudopatients of faking insanity—the real patients guessed that the imposters were actually professors or reporters who were in the hospital to conduct a study! ■

# Is the Death Penalty Only a Vehicle for Revenge?
## An Ardent Abolitionist States His Case

Whenever I articulate my opposition to the death penalty, I feel like a voice in the wilderness. More than 75% of all Americans favor the death penalty, and the remaining 25% would probably be willing to make an exception if it meant eliminating the Ted Bundys of the world. In fact, the United States has the dubious distinction of being the only remaining Western nation not to have abolished the death penalty for civil homicide.

Some proponents of capital punishment assert that legislators should enact death penalty laws because it is the will of the people. Well, it is true that the majority of Americans support capital punishment—BUT ONLY if they are not given an alternative that they like better. When they are offered an option to capital punishment like life without parole, their support for the death penalty drops to 50%—even lower when you throw in compensating the victim's family.

Unfortunately, many of our citizens really aren't informed enough about criminal justice policy to make a rational decision about crime and punishment. In one recent survey, pollsters found that only a fraction of the residents of Massachusetts—about 3%—even knew that the Commonwealth's penalty for first-degree murder was life without parole. One third of all Massachusetts citizens said they believed such offenders would be out of prison in less than 10 years; another 11% said they had no idea at all what happened to first-degree murderers in the state.

But the reason underlying much of the support of executions, according to a recent survey conducted for *ABC News* and the *Washington Post*, is usually revenge or retribution. Americans believe that the most serious crimes deserve the most severe punishment. As the Old Testament points out, "Thou shalt give life for life, eye for eye, tooth for tooth."

And I admit, it's not hard to understand why revenge seems sweet. People are fed up with violent crime, believing that it is out of control and of epidemic proportions. They want to do something about it.

Many idolize Bernard Goetz, the so-called subway vigilante, because he refused to passively accept his victimization. The same appeal can be seen cinematically in Mel Gibson's character in *Ransom* and in Sylvester Stallone's portrayal of Rambo and Rocky. Whether or not I agree with the extremity of the public reaction, I can understand why Bundy's execution by the state of Florida was seen by many as a cause for celebration. The world lost one of its most despicable killers.

The arguments for the death penalty, however, typically fall outside the realm of empirical inquiry. Instead, they are often emotionally charged, arguing that convicted killers deserve to die or that "getting even" is valuable as a measure of psychological compensation for victims and society. As an abolitionist, however, I rest my entire case on the weight of economic and social issues that can be demonstrated by empirical inquiry. These three important issues involve cost, deterrence, and protection.

Many people ask why we should spend hard-earned taxpayer money to imprison a murderer when we could just as easily execute him at much lower cost. But the fixed costs of running a maximum-security prison are little affected by the presence of a few additional inmates serving life sentences for first-degree murder. The warden still has to be paid and the heat still has to be kept on. Moreover, because of the lengthy appeals process required by the Supreme Court in capital cases, it actually costs less to imprison a killer than to execute one. In Florida, for example, the average cost of a case that results in execution is $3.2 million, whereas the estimated cost of imprisonment for 40 years is slightly more than $500,000. And to those who argue, "If it costs so much to carry out the appeals process, then take him out back and string him up," consider the number of errors that have been made under less stringent requirements: Since 1900, 139 people have been sent to death who were later proven innocent. Twenty-three of them were exonerated only after the executions had been carried out. In addition, the typical length of imprisonment between sentencing and execution is actually only 3 years, not the 11 years that Ted Bundy manipulated out of the court system.

Proponents of the death penalty also claim that it deters violent criminals. They believe we need to execute murderers to send messages to potential killers that, if they can't control their murderous behavior, the same thing will happen to them.

Yet the death penalty has little if any effect on killings. In a study of 14 nations in which the death penalty was eliminated, criminologists Dane Archer and Rosemary Gartner report, for example, that abolition was followed more often than not by a reduction in national homicide rates. For example, homicide dropped 59% in Finland, 30% in Italy, 63% in Sweden, and 46% in Switzerland. In only 5 of these 14 countries did homicide increase at all. Even more ironically, research conducted by criminologist William Bowers suggests that the murder rate actually rises for a short period of time after the killer has been executed, producing what he calls a "brutalization effect." That is, would-be murderers apparently identify more with the state executioner than they do with the inmate.

The third argument, of course, is that capital punishment protects society by guaranteeing that killers like Charles Manson will never be paroled. And certainly, capital punishment would make sure that particular murderers never kill again. But before I support the death penalty, I want to know whether an alternative exists for protecting society—for making sure that a killer isn't granted another opportunity—without taking human life. If the alternative in response to a brutal, hideous murder is life imprisonment with parole eligibility, then I am indeed in favor of the death penalty. If, however, the alternative is a life sentence without the possibility of ever being paroled, then capital punishment becomes unnecessary for the protection of society, and I am therefore against it.

In fact, I cringe whenever I hear that Charles Manson is being considered for parole, because I know what people will say: "The criminal justice system is soft on murderers. We should be executing those who commit heinous crimes." Actually, Charles Manson did receive the death penalty. But in 1972, the Supreme Court struck down capital punishment because it was being applied in an uneven, capricious manner. At that point, any murderer on death row was instead given the next most severe sentence under state law. In California, that sentence was a life sentence with parole eligibility. As a result, Charles Manson was then eligible for parole after serving only 7 years.

A series of rulings by the Supreme Court in 1976 paved the way for states to restore the death penalty but only when applied under strict guidelines. In some states (for example, California), those convicted of murder continue to become eligible for parole after serving several years in prison; but if the court adds the "special circumstances provision," the only possible sentences are either death or life imprisonment without parole eligibility.

Most states now have special circumstances statutes for heinous crimes, such as multiple murder or murder with rape. In some states (e.g., Massachusetts), all first-degree murderers are ineligible for parole, so that no special statute is required. Under such conditions, the death penalty is unnecessary as a means for protecting society from vicious killers because we can instead lock them up and throw away the key.

Actually, many proponents of the death penalty raise the issues of cost, deterrence, and protection of society only to rationalize what essentially is a thirst for revenge. This can be seen most clearly in the public response to heinous crimes.

In December 1987, Ronald Gene Simmons brutally murdered 16 people in Russellville, Arkansas, in the largest family massacre in American history. When the residents of Russellville learned that Simmons had suffocated the young children in his family and that he had had an incestuous relationship with his married daughter, cries for the death penalty were heard loud and clear throughout Arkansas. In 1989, Simmons was convicted of multiple murder and sentenced to die by means of lethal injection. Similarly, in October 1989, a young pregnant woman from Reading, Massachusetts was shot to death by her husband, Charles Stuart. Public outrage quickly took the form of demands for Massachusetts legislators to enact a death penalty statute.

Florida certainly did get a measure of self-satisfaction by electrocuting serial killer Ted Bundy; the same can be said for the state of Illinois when it executed John Wayne Gacy, the notorious serial killer, in 1994. For many Americans, the opportunity to get even with a serial killer is reason enough to apply the death penalty. But for those few who instead believe that capital punishment can be justified only to the extent that it protects society's members or serves as an effective deterrent, then execution by the state is cruel and unnecessary punishment. In a civilized society, our best defense against "wild animals" is to lock them in cages so they can't get to the rest of us. ∎

# Animal Cruelty and Human Violence
Is There a Connection?
*with Arnold Arluke*

In the suburbs of Jackson, Mississippi, 16-year-old Luke Woodham allegedly killed two girls and injured seven other students before being subdued by a Pearl High School administrator. Earlier that day, Woodham's mother was found stabbed to death, and he was charged with the murder.

These killings have sparked nationwide attention in part because of bizarre plans by Woodham, a self-proclaimed Satanist, and his fellow "cult" members to lay siege to the school by igniting explosives, cutting telephone lines, and killing various people. A far more common event could have warned authorities that Woodham was ready to explode, but nobody paid attention to it.

More than 6 months earlier, the defendant and one of his friends repeatedly beat Woodham's dog, wrapped it in bags, set it on fire, and threw it into a pond. Woodham ostensibly wrote, "I made my first kill . . . The victim was a loved one, my dear dog Sparkle . . . I will never forget the howl she made. It sounded almost human."

Research strongly suggests that understanding the causes and consequences of violence toward animals may be important in the effort to fight crime against humans. A link has long been suspected between cruelty to animals and human violence. In the 1960s, for example, psychiatrist John Macdonald first suggested that those individuals who later become homicidal begin in childhood by torturing small animals. Subsequent research on violent prisoners and abusive domestic partners supported Macdonald's position.

Indeed, a 3-year study we recently conducted with the Massachusetts Society for the Prevention of Cruelty to Animals examined the relationship between violence against animals and crime in the general population. We discovered that people who abused animals were five times more likely than those who did not to commit violent crimes against people—to assault, rape, or rob them.

Surprisingly, animal abuse was found to be linked with many types of nonviolent crimes as well. Abusers were four times more likely than nonabusers to commit property crimes and three times more likely to be arrested for drug-related offenses and disorderly conduct.

What can be done to reduce animal abuse and to recognize its value as a warning sign of future violence? We urge professionals—district attorneys, judges, police officers, doctors, social workers, teachers, and ministers—to take appropriate measures. Every year thousands of animals around the country are reported as victims of malicious cruelty. Recently, a resident of Manatee County, Florida admitted beating to death a neighbor's 11-year-old Rottweiler with a 2-foot club; in Iowa, three teenagers were brought to trial for bludgeoning to death 16 cats in an animal shelter.

If these crimes were committed against children, the abusers would likely face stiff penalties in court, but not so in one of the animal offenses. Even in the most extreme cases, a majority of the animal abusers are not found guilty in court. Most don't even get to trial. When they do, they typically get a slap on the wrist. In some states, only 1 in 10 of those convicted receive jail sentences. And fines are minimal when imposed, averaging $132.

Most important, incidents of animal cruelty are typically viewed as isolated crimes, having no relationship to other human behavior such as violence against people. The attitude among criminal justice personnel too frequently seems to be: "Suppose we make a concerted effort to wipe out animal cruelty—So what? When the money is spent, we will still be left fighting rape, murder, assault, burglary, and drug abuse."

There is strong public support to take these measures. According to a recent national survey, 71% of adults favor making animal abuse a felony. Eighty-one percent approve strengthening the enforcement of cruelty laws. About 83% favor teachers, social workers, animal welfare officers, and law enforcement officials sharing information on juveniles who abuse animals as an early warning sign of criminal behavior. And 75% support the establishment of a system for tracking adult animal cruelty offenders as a tool for identifying other kinds of likely violent offenses.

Of course, not every child who tortures animals grows up to become a killer. Yet, animal abuse is clearly a warning sign that deserves to be taken seriously in order to intervene before it's too late. The lesson is clear enough: By taking animal cruelty more seriously, we might help ourselves. ■

# America's Youngsters Are Responsible for Church Burnings
## It's Neither the Klan Nor the White Aryan Resistance

It is tempting to regard the recent wave of church burnings across the country as some kind of conspiracy involving white supremacist extremists. Yet the evidence suggests something much worse. Most of these racially inspired arsons seem to be the work of America's young people.

Collectively, scapegoating frequently takes the form of "protest by proxy," in which innocent victims substitute for the real source of economic hardship. As growing income inequality continues to take its toll, those Americans for whom the American Dream seems out of reach derive little satisfaction from blaming vague abstractions like global competition, corporate downsizing, or automation. Scapegoating minorities puts a human face on what otherwise would be a nebulous and unintelligible enemy.

Black Americans have always made especially effective scapegoats. Not only were they powerless to strike back effectively, but they had adequate visibility as well. Until 1930, the frequency with which blacks in the South were lynched increased as the value of Southern cotton declined. Black Americans were routinely blamed for downward economic fluctuations that might rationally have been attributed more to changes in the weather than to human intervention.

Criminologist Jack McDevitt and I have studied hundreds of serious crimes directed against individuals because they are different with respect to race, religion, national origin, or sexual orientation. If the recent string of church burnings is at all typical of hate attacks generally, then very few of them are being committed by the members of organized hate groups. Instead, almost two thirds of the arsons will probably turn out to be thrill crimes committed by young people who go out looking to stir up a little excitement at someone else's expense. These youngsters aren't getting along at home, are doing poorly in school, or have dead-end jobs. Typically they hate themselves as much as they hate their victims and are looking for someone to blame for their personal problems.

Though few arrests have been made, it thus far appears that young people have been disproportionately involved in the church burnings. Two weeks ago, a 13-year-old girl was arrested and charged for an act of arson which destroyed the Matthews Murkland Presbyterian Church in Charlotte, North Carolina. Three men in their early 20s were prime suspects in the burning of the Lighthouse Prayer Church in Greenville, Texas. Last year, two boys, ages nine and 10, were charged with destroying Life Christian Assembly Church in North Charleston, South Carolina. A 17-year-old was charged in the burning of Pleasant Hill Baptist Church in Roberson County, North Carolina.

The good news about thrill hate attacks is that their perpetrators are generally not hardened hatemongers but only naive young adults and teenagers who hardly understand Nazi ideology or Klan slogans. Most of them don't know the KKK from the White Aryan Resistance. With a creative response including education and community service, we might reach many of these youthful offenders in time to turn their lives around and make them into productive citizens.

The bad news is that the string of church burnings reflects a more general trend toward escalating levels of bigotry and intolerance among America's youths. Too many of them feel important only to the extent that they are able to inflict pain and suffering on people who are different in terms of race, religion, or sexual orientation. So they burn, bash, and desecrate in order to feel superior.

In response to hurtful acts of intolerance, our mainstream leaders should send an unequivocal message that they will simply not tolerate intolerance. Strong hate crime laws for repeat offenders is, in this regard, an indispensable tool. Creative alternative sentencing for youthful first offenders—education, community service, and victim restitution—is also essential.

But the most effective approach by far would be to offer our bigoted youngsters some hope for the future. We must reach them with healthy alternatives to prejudice and violence, giving them some reason to feel good about themselves without terrorizing their neighbors. ■

■ **FOCUS** *Suggestions for Further Reading*

In the introduction to this section, I discussed the work of French sociologist Émile Durkheim. The frequency with which he appears in this small book should suggest just how much the work of Durkheim has influenced the direction of sociology. Durkheim's views of crime are found in *The Rules of Sociological Method* (1966).

Concerning "Is the Death Penalty Only a Vehicle for Revenge?" my argument relies on numerous studies by criminologists, most of whom find little or no support for the death penalty. For two major studies of capital punishment, read William J. Bowers's books—*Executions in America* (1974) and *Legal Homicide* (1984). Dane Archer and Rosemary Gartner, in their important book titled *Violence and Crime in Cross-National Perspective* (1984), provide cross-national evidence. They found a reduction in homicide for most of the countries in which the death penalty was abolished. For a systematic examination of capital murder cases in which individuals have been falsely accused, see Micheal Radelet and his colleagues (1992). A comprehensive overview of various aspects of the death penalty can be found in William Schabas (1997), *The International Sourcebook on Capital Punishment*.

My snapshot about the death penalty takes a controversial position. I first raised the issue of value-free sociology in the introduction to this book; it should come as no surprise to see it again—especially in discussing how to deal with crime. In 1918, Max Weber gave a lecture at Munich University concerning the importance of value-free sociology. You can find his speech reprinted in *Max Weber: Essays in Sociology*, edited by H. H. Gerth and C. Wright Mills (1946). For a different point of view regarding the place of values in sociological analysis, read "Whose Side Are We On?" by Howard S. Becker, in *Social Problems* (1967). He argues that sociological research is *always* biased, never value-free; in fact, every sociologist has a responsibility to take sides in support of important values and concerns.

For a perspective and interesting examination of the sociology of animals, read Arnold Arluke and Clinton R. Sanders's award-winning book, *Regarding Animals* (1996). The sadism in many crimes against animals may be the link with similar acts of violence committed against humans. Two books seem especially relevant to the topic. First, Jack Katz examines the subjective experiences of doing crime in his fascinating book *Seductions of Crime: Moral and Sensual Attractions of Doing Evil* (1988). He looks beyond the practical and senseless motivational veneer of criminal behavior and focuses instead on its moral and sensual rewards. For a controversial and important explanation for criminal behavior, read Michael Gottfredson and Travis Hirschi's *A General Theory of Crime* (1990). Gottfredson and Hirschi present evidence for the position that an essential element in criminality is an absence of self-control, usually learned early in life. This is a factor that may very well be present in crimes against both animals and humans. For a discussion of animal abuse as a symptom of violence proneness in serial killers and mass murderers, read Jack Levin and James A. Fox, *Mass Murder: America's Growing Menace* (1991).

In "America's Youngsters Are Responsible for Church Burnings," the blame for the recent rash of church burnings—especially arsons against black churches—is placed squarely on our youths. From the beginning, it appeared that many, if not most, were committed by teenagers who got a thrill out of causing trouble for the members of another racial group. Only in a few cases were organized hate groups involved. This finding is true of hate crimes in general, most of which are committed by teenagers who go out in a group to vandalize, bash, or assault people who are different. For a typology of hate crimes from which my analysis of church burnings was derived, see Jack Levin and Jack McDevitt, *Hate Crimes: The Rising Tide of Bigotry and Bloodshed* (1993).

Throughout this section, we have emphasized criminal behavior as a form of deviance. In closing this section, let me point out, once again, that crime is only one form of deviance and that deviance is actually a much broader concept. Many sociologists who specialize in deviance aren't primarily interested in crime at all and instead study various forms of deviant behavior, such as mental illness or physical disability.

In "Fat Chance in a Slim World," we are also told that, throughout history, people who would be considered overweight by Americans in the 1990s were instead respected, admired, and regarded as attractive. Rather than the epitome of feminine beauty, even Cleopatra of ancient Egypt was fat by our standards!

In contrast, Americans who are overweight by conventional standards are stigmatized. Specifically, they are treated as lacking in moral fiber and character. As more "food for thought" about this topic, pick up Kim Chernin's interesting book *The Obsession* (1981). She suggests that women's acceptance of society's increasing demand for females to be thin reflects cultural pressure for women to dislike their bodies. For Chernin, rigid dieting and boyish fashions are forms of rejection of feminine power and equality. My snapshot depends a good deal on Chernin and on Marcia Millman's excellent sociological treatise about being fat in America, *Such a Pretty Face* (1980). For the classic sociological treatment of the presentation of "spoiled" self, see Erving Goffman's *Stigma: Notes on the Management of Spoiled Identity* (1963). While reading Goffman, think about the influence that being fat or skinny or very short or very tall can have on a child's self-image.

Goffman has also written extensively about mental hospitals. His book titled *Asylums* (1958) is a classic in the field. David Rosenhan's excellent study of normal people gaining entrance into a mental hospital and then asking to be discharged is reported in his 1973 article "On Being Sane in Insane Places," appearing in *Science*. For an excellent discussion of the social conditions implicated in mental illnesses such as depression and anxiety, read *Social Causes of Psychological Distress* (1989), written by John Mirowsky and Catherine Ross. ■

■ **DEVELOPING IDEAS** *About Deviance*

1. Writing topic: Max Weber urged sociologists to attempt to be objective, even when their personal views were being contradicted. Gun control is a controversial issue—there are many proponents on both sides. In writing, state your own personal opinion—either for or against the restriction of firearms as a national policy. Then, in a short essay, defend the point of view that opposes your own.

2. Research topic: Every year, the U.S. Department of Justice publishes the Uniform Crime Reports for the United States. In *Crime in the United States*, you will find a number of different statistics concerning the serious crimes reported to the FBI by local police departments. This book is easily available in libraries or from the U.S. Government Printing Office. Using *Crime in the United States* for a recent year, find monthly variations in murder and verify that murder rates peak during July, August, and Decem-

ber. Now, do the same for property crimes such as larceny, theft, and burglary. Do these offenses also peak during the relatively cold month of December? Why or why not? Explain how the social climate may have more influence than the weather on monthly variations in homicide. Do you think that the social climate has the same effect on property crimes?

3. Research topic: Based on public opinion surveys, we know that most Americans favor the death penalty. But we also know that support for capital punishment decreases if people see an alternative that protects society just as well. For example, in a 1994 survey of Massachusetts citizens, William J. Bowers found that 54% prefer life without parole over the death penalty. Now, it's your turn. In a paper-and-pencil questionnaire, ask 20 students to indicate whether they support or oppose capital punishment. Now, also ask the supporters of the death penalty to indicate whether they would support or oppose it under the following conditions: (a) if life imprisonment were the only alternative sentence available; (b) if life imprisonment without parole eligibility were the only alternative sentence available; (c) if life without hope—that is, life imprisonment without parole eligibility, pardon, or commutation of sentence—were the only alternative available; or (d) if life imprisonment without parole eligibility plus victim restitution were the only alternative sentence available. What do your results indicate about protection of society as a motivation for supporting the death penalty?

4. Research topic: With your instructor's assistance, commit an act of deviance to see how others respond to you. Select an act that is neither illegal nor unethical. Also, make sure that your deviant behavior will not affect the way you are treated by others on a permanent basis! Because it isn't always so easy to think of a safe act of deviance, let me suggest one. Simply mark your forehead with a meaningless symbol—for example, two blue and red circles. Then, walk on campus and observe the reactions (or lack of reactions). Do strangers and friends respond differently to you? Finally, try the same experiment, but this time walk on campus with two other students whose foreheads have been painted like yours. Do you notice a difference in the way you are treated? What do you think people assume when they encounter three students wearing the same unknown symbol?

5. Research topic: Interview an individual who seems to be stigmatized because of his or her appearance (someone considered fat, short, tall, unattractive, and so on). In your interview, try to determine at what age your respondent first remembers being different. Have your respondent indicate the specific ways in which he or she has been discriminated against—at work, on dates, at school. Also try to discover how he or she manages the stigma (denial or avoidance?). Note: Please be careful not to approach a stigmatized person in a hurtful or insensitive way. You might want to place an ad in your college newspaper asking for volunteers who have been labeled as too short, too tall, or too fat. Or you might invite volunteers from among your classmates. It may even be possible to locate an organization to which stigmatized people belong—for example, Little People of America or the National Association to Aid Fat Americans. In any case, it is obviously important to use extreme sensitivity in locating a potential respondent.
6. Writing topic: Name a group in American society, other than fat people, whose members have been stigmatized. How do you think they would be treated in some other culture? Why?
7. Research topic: Walk around for one day as a fat person to see how other people treat you. With the help of a friend, put on more than a few pounds—literally put on weight by wearing large clothing and padding yourself in a realistic way. Then, take written notes as to any differences you detect in the reactions of others. ■

# PART SIX

## Social Inequality

"Back in the good old days," the gap between the haves and the have-nots was attributed solely to a lack of effort on the part of the individual. We still like to think of the United States as the land of equal opportunity and are loath to admit that the structure of our society facilitates inequality. The physical gap between the "junker" car on the right and the high-priced sports car on the left may be small, yet the gap between the lives of these two men is immense. Being white and male was never a guarantee of success, but today, more than ever, racial differences and sexual inequality only work to compound class inequality. Although they share some demographic characteristics, these two men live profoundly different lives because of their class differences.

"Can you spare some change for a cup of coffee, mister?" I never know what to do when I am confronted by a panhandler asking for a handout, especially if he looks like he's been drinking. If I give him what he wants, I might only be supplying him with his next drink of booze and his next hangover. But if I don't give him anything, I feel guilty. Who knows, maybe he hasn't eaten in 3 days and my small contribution will keep him going until the next handout comes along.

Homeless people in the streets of our major cities represent an extreme example of *social inequality*—the unequal distribution of wealth, power, and prestige among the members of society. At the other end of that distribution, there are entertainers and professional athletes who earn millions of dollars a year, enjoy tremendous popularity, and have a great deal of pull. In between the panhandler and the famous ballplayer, most of us fall.

Clearly, we are not a classless society. In fact, social inequality in America is highly structured and passed from one generation to another. This characteristic of social inequality is known as *social stratification*. In fact, social inequality is definitely stratified. Sociologists have been able to identify a number of different social classes whose members share similar occupational positions, opportunities, attitudes, and lifestyles—an upper class containing the wealthiest and most powerful people in America, an upper middle class consisting of the families of business executives and professionals who have high income, a lower middle class consisting of average-income Americans, a working class containing primarily blue-collar workers, and a lower class consisting of the "disreputable poor."

*Life chances* is Max Weber's term referring to an individual's probability of securing the "good things of life." Sociologists are well aware that an individual's life chances definitely vary by social class. Regardless of their intelligence and steadfastness, people who are born into a low social class will likely benefit less from society's opportunities than people born into a higher social class. Members of lower classes are *less* likely to vote, obtain favors from politicians, go to college, receive adequate public services, be in good physical and mental health, have decent working conditions, or feel they have control over their everyday lives. They are *more* likely to give birth out of wedlock, grow up in single-parent families, be arrested and imprisoned after committing a crime, and die at an early age.

Many observers have suggested that the gap between rich and poor has widened over the period of the last decade or so. Clearly, there are now more homeless people on the streets of our major cities and more middle-class families whose members have "skidded" in terms of social class. In "The Economic Escalator," we find that intergenerational mobility seems to be in a downward direction. Consequently, millions of young people have begun to question the validity of the American Dream. Young adults have been particularly hard hit. As a result, they are staying in school longer, delaying their marriage plans, and moving back in with their parents.

Social inequality varies by gender, race, and age. African Americans continue to be disproportionately represented in poverty. Affirmative action legislation may have helped create a large and viable black middle class, but it has hardly touched the lives of the members of the black underclass who continue to live in permanent poverty. In our postindustrial society, we lack the jobs that could propel young black males out of the underclass. And where such jobs do exist, they tend to be low-paying jobs that lead nowhere. In "Another Crisis in Black and White? The Coming Race War in America," I suggest the possibility that such economic conditions may help precipitate a dangerous conflict between black and white Americans.

In addition, American women continue to earn less than their male counterparts. Moreover, when both husband and wife hold full-time jobs, it is usually the working woman who is expected to do the household chores and child rearing as well. She continues to be the main source of advice and guidance for her children and the one who is held responsible for cleaning and cooking. Perhaps this fact of life helps explain the American female's disadvantage on the job: Because of the extra burden placed on her shoulders, the working woman is often unable to make the same commitment to her career that her husband can.

In the early 1980s, we were in the grip of a recession, and older Americans suffered more than their share of economic hardship. Some were eating dog food to survive. Perhaps fewer elders are now in critical economic condition, but their image continues to give them problems. In "Images of Aging," I suggest that the old stereotype that all older people are poor, sickly, and incompetent has been joined by a new stereotype that they are *also* powerful and wealthy—perhaps too powerful and wealthy for their own good. The new view may turn out to be particularly dangerous, inspiring conflict between the generations for increasingly scarce economic resources. Indeed, there already exist political pressure organizations designed to minimize the influence of older people in the areas of social security and health care. Americans for Generational Equity represents the interests of young people, and the American Association of Boomers represents the interests of middle-aged Americans.

Another segment of the population of the United States that suffered during the 1980s was residents of rural areas—farmers, ranchers, miners, and people in the timber industry who were hard hit by recession and never quite came out of it. It is no coincidence that civilian militia groups have received a good deal of support from people in the rural areas of the country. Not only do many of them feel frustrated, they also feel ignored by the rest of society.

The United States is in the midst of a possibly unprecedented period of immigration—and not everyone is delighted. In "Immigrants Create Jobs for Americans," Bill Leong and I present a viewpoint that is apparently at odds with that popularly held; namely, we argue that immigrants make life better, not worse, for native-born citizens. Another point of view entirely is represented in the numerous acts of violence perpetrated against newcomers not only in the United States but around the world, as increasing numbers of frustrated individuals look for someone to blame for their bad economic situation. Using the framework laid out by sociologist Lewis Coser in his modern classic *The Functions of Social Conflict*, it is also possible to raise the possibility that immigrant bashing helps protect the leaders of a society from the unmitigated hostility of its citizens. ∎

# The Economic Escalator
## Americans on Their Way Down

The term *downward mobility* is used to characterize the economic plight of an entire generation of middle-class Americans who are slipping and sliding their way down the socioeconomic ladder. Forget about the short-term effects of the recession of 1991. According to political analyst Kevin Phillips, the culprit is an economic trend that began in the 1970s or 1980s and will likely continue indefinitely.

The rich really have been getting much richer—and apparently doing so at the expense of poor and middle-income Americans who have seen their status evaporate. Through at least the last decade, the biggest losers have been blacks, Latinos, young men, female heads of households, farmers, and steelworkers, but almost everyone else has also suffered to some extent.

In a shift away from manufacturing toward services, we have been transformed into a postindustrial society. In 1959, production of goods represented some 60% of all American employment, but by 1985, this figure had dropped to only 26%. The overwhelming majority of Americans are now employed in the service sector of the economy. During this transitional period, many new jobs were created, but in the main, these were poorly paid and provided few opportunities for upward mobility. Large numbers of Americans were forced to take a substantial drop in pay and, therefore, in their way of life.

Economist Jeffrey Madrick associates reduced worker wages in the United States with the fact that our economy is no longer growing at a healthy rate. Beginning in 1973, the American economy grew much more slowly than it had on average since the Civil War. Over a 20-year period, therefore, our country has produced $20 trillion less in goods and services than it would have had we maintained our historically high rate of growth.

Consistent with this view, Phillips suggests that the widening gap between rich and poor may have been encouraged by national economic policies of the 1980s, a period that represented a strong reversal of almost four decades of downward income redistribution. At the upper end of our class system, the after-tax proportion of income for the wealthiest 1% of Americans climbed from 7% in 1977 to 11%

in 1990. Even when adjusted for inflation, the number of millionaires doubled between the late 1970s and the late 1980s, resulting in a record 1 million households reporting a net worth of at least $1 million.

For families on lower rungs of the socioeconomic ladder, however, living standards have deteriorated. Since 1977, the average after-tax family income of the bottom 10% of Americans declined 10.5% in current dollars. Recent government statistics reported by the U.S. Census Bureau indicate that this trend is likely to continue: During 1996, families in the bottom fifth of the income distribution nationally saw their incomes drop an additional 2%. But families in the top 20% gained another 2%. According to a recent study by Professor Timothy Smeeding of Syracuse University, the percentage of U.S. children living in poverty rose from less than 15% in 1978 to 20% today. Compared with seven other industrial countries (Sweden, West Germany, Australia, Canada, Britain, France, and The Netherlands), the United States has the dubious distinction of being the most unequal. That is, we have more poverty and fewer people who are middle class.

Growing income inequality has already been linked with a worsening of our most stubborn and perplexing social ailments. Professor Henry Miller of the University of California notes that homelessness is a growing problem in our major cities—a problem that is not susceptible to easy solutions. He suggests that we were previously able as a society to assimilate many of the homeless into the military or industry. In today's economy, however, those who lack education or marketable skills remain permanently unemployed or take dead-end jobs. What is more, in the process of converting inexpensive rooming houses into high-priced condominiums for the affluent, the gentrification of urban areas during the 1980s forced even more of the poverty stricken onto the streets.

According to *American Demographics,* young adults have been particularly hard hit by downward mobility. As a result, they are taking longer to finish school, living for a longer period of time with their parents or other relatives, and delaying their plans to marry. Young married couples are today less likely to own their own homes. Many return to live with their parents.

Comparing their worsening economic circumstances with those of their parents, millions of young people have begun to question the validity of the American Dream and are less optimistic about the future. Called "selfish," "passive," and "ultraconservative" by those who remember the liberal activism of the prosperous 1960s, many young adults are merely trying to maintain or improve their standard of living. In the face of an erosion in their incomes, they frequently regard tax increases as a burden they cannot afford.

The continuing trends away from manufacturing and toward inequality between rich and poor are, of course, far from inevitable. But a reversal would necessitate a major commitment on the part of political leaders, business, and the public, who recognize the urgency of finding a solution. The urban underclass is now larger than it was during the turbulent 1960s, when our major cities were burning. Throughout the 1990s, there have been dozens of violent disturbances in cities around the nation. Some predict riots of earthquake proportions within 2 to 3 years in at least four major cities: New York, Chicago, Los Angeles, and Miami. At that point, there will undoubtedly be widespread support for making essential changes in our economy. The real question is one of timing: Will we be too late? ■

# Images of Aging
Are the Elderly Too Powerful?

Several years ago, 80-year-old Clara Peller achieved overnight fame for her line in a Wendy's ad, "Where's the beef?" Peller's comic portrayal of a cantankerous old lady reflects a familiar stereotype: Older people are seen as entering a second childhood in which they become bossy, irritable, feeble, and possibly weakened in intellect and make large, unreasonable demands on others. With low incomes and high health costs, elderly consumers are seen as especially concerned about finding the "beef," about getting good value for their money.

Studies of age stereotyping conducted over the past 50 years show that this image of aging has been widely accepted. Gerontologists' research among graduate students of psychology in the 1950s shows that most believed that old people are set in their ways, walk slowly, have poor coordination, are bossy, and like to doze. These results have been duplicated in more recent research. A 1988 study by William C. Levin reported in *Research on Aging* showed that Americans characterize older people as less intelligent, competent, healthy, active, creative, attractive, reliable, energetic, flexible, educated, wealthy, and socially involved than younger people.

Most of my students routinely overestimate the percentage of the elderly who live below the poverty line or in nursing homes. For example, the average estimate was that 37% of all Americans 65 years or older are now residing in a nursing home, while the actual figure is only 4%.

Surprisingly, these same students also overestimated the percentage of senators, judges, and former presidents who were at least 65 and the proportion of billionaires, CEOs of major corporations, and corporate stockholders who are elderly. The same students who were unrealistic about poverty and dependence exaggerated the wealth and power of the elderly: Less than 5% of major American corporations are actually headed by a CEO who is 65 or older, but the average estimated by the students was 43%.

In this latter stereotype, older people are often seen as powerful and rich—perhaps too powerful and rich for their own good.

Traditionally, older people were blamed for their own plight; their poverty and dependence were regarded as an inevitable part of the life cycle. In the new view, however, the aged are seen as having disproportionate influence in the government, as having garnered too large a share of the country's economic resources, and as responsible for a national debt of unprecedented proportions and for health care costs that seem to be out of control.

The former view long justified encouraging the elderly to disengage from work, despite evidence that older workers are as productive as their younger counterparts. The new stereotype is potentially even more dangerous. It justifies organizing against the interests of the elderly, cutting the government expenditures that benefit them, perhaps even eliminating Social Security, and reducing efforts to keep the aged alive. In this view, since the elderly have so much wealth and political clout, they do not need the help of younger Americans.

Some have already begun to exploit the new stereotype. In politics, the interests of the elderly and the young have been pitted against one another as though they were in essential conflict—a substitute for the real battle that is so carefully avoided—that of the poor and middle class against the rich. Americans for Generational Equity (AGE), for example, argues that the status of the elderly has greatly improved at the expense of the well-being of the young. The leaders of AGE cite statistics showing high rates of poverty among children, a decline in real income among baby boomers, and a massive federal debt. AGE blames the elderly for consuming too much of the national budget and enjoying increases in Social Security benefits, while inflation-adjusted wages for the rest of the population have declined.

Even more disturbing is the extent to which this perception may be influencing medical personnel who make life and death decisions. Studies have shown that emergency room personnel tend to expend greater effort resuscitating younger patients. Colorado's former governor Richard Lamm said that the elderly "have a duty to die" because of the financial cost of health care needed to prolong the lives of the elderly. According to Lamm, it might cost too much to keep them alive.

Now the Clara Peller image is of someone who has found the beef and refuses to share it with her grandchildren. Older Americans deserve a better commercial. ∎

# An Apple Pie and an Open Mind
## My Visit to a Patriot Potluck

Just prior to the opening days of Timothy McVeigh's trial for his role in the deadly 1995 Oklahoma City bombing, militia groups were back in the news. McVeigh apparently had been associated with a civilian militia in Kingman, Arizona. His "bible" was the infamous *Turner Diaries*, a fictionalized account of a coming civil war, in which revolutionaries bring down the federal government by bombing federal buildings and disrupting public utilities.

I recently attended a "Patriot Potluck" attended by militia members, survivalists, and assorted right-wing political discontents. We met on a Saturday in an obscure dinner theater building just north of Boston. I brought an apple pie and an open mind.

For the entire morning and much of the afternoon, I joined with members of the Patriot Movement as they swapped ideas, listened attentively to a parade of speakers, and lunched on pasta salad, sandwiches, and my apple pie. Along the sides of the room, vendors hawked their anti-New World Order T-shirts and conspiratorial literature. In unison, we sang patriotic songs and recited the Pledge of Allegiance.

I confess feeling just a little nervous to be among people who are totally convinced that our federal government has been taken over by communists. I am not now, nor have I ever been, a member of any militia group, the John Birch Society, or the Pat Buchanan fan club. I decided to attend this gathering of political extremists in order to learn more about the militia movement, its members and its causes. It never occurred to me, however, that I would learn even more about what is wrong with mainstream American institutions.

Civilian militias have long been linked, at least in the public mind, with violence and bigotry—with tragedies and near-tragedies at Ruby Ridge; Jordan, Montana; the Atlanta Olympics; and Oklahoma City. According to the stereotyped image, *all* militia members are nothing more than a collection of gun-loving, bomb-throwing hatemongers and terrorists.

That is why I was so surprised when the 75 men, women, and children who attended this meeting seemed so hospitable and friendly, even innocuous. From a distance, they could easily have been mistaken for a group of bridge players or a convention of social workers. Admittedly, I did hear a racist comment from a speaker and an anti-Jewish remark from one member of the audience. But, then, I also met a few dedicated members of the movement who were themselves Black or Jewish.

I was also impressed by the utter boredom of their speeches. Through a 5-hour procession of speakers, I heard much less about guns and bombs than about economic survival. Speaker after speaker talked about money—about how to defeat the IRS through Common Law courts, how to withdraw from the Social Security system, the impact of free trade on the unemployment rate, and how to avoid going into debt. I got the strong impression that these were Americans—many from rural backgrounds—who had suffered through hard economic times and were looking for some way to explain their shared predicament. Their response was to blame the federal government, communists, the UN, and international bankers.

Any group of Americans who believes that the enemy has surreptitiously taken over the White House, Congress, and the Supreme Court is potentially dangerous. These so-called patriots are no exception. But to treat the entire militia movement as consisting merely of a collection of crazies who deserve to be carted off to an asylum is just as dangerous. Many of the issues addressed at the Patriot Potluck I attended were every bit as much the concerns of conventional, middle-of-the-road Americans who struggle daily to survive in the face of global competition and growing income inequality. They may not join a militia or stockpile weapons in anticipation of a revolution—they may not even attend a potluck meeting to voice their anxieties—but they are nevertheless convinced that the government is no longer working on behalf of ordinary citizens.

There is a natural tendency for government to respond to extremism with repressive measures, which give even more power to law enforcement agencies in their efforts to investigate and infiltrate marginal groups. In the short run, such measures might prevent a violent episode or two. In the long run, however, they reduce the individual freedoms of all Americans and only push potentially dangerous groups underground. In the end, members of fringe organizations, already convinced that the government is out to get them, will be even more paranoid and delusional. As a result, they may actually become the menace they are perceived to be.

Of course, Americans of good will should be vigilant in response to a growing threat of terrorism perpetrated by our own citizens. But if we are careful to look past the stereotyped images of the Patriot Movement that frequently pass for reality, we might learn something about our country that needs to be repaired and is within our power to change: the need to work together as a nation in order to create a sense of trust and social responsibility that transcends the differences that divide us. If we are successful in this regard, the Patriot Movement will probably wither and die of its own irrelevancy. But if we are not, then today's extremism could easily become tomorrow's version of moderation. ∎

# Immigrants Create Jobs for Americans
Americans Create Trouble for Newcomers
*with William J. Leong*

According to a study issued recently by the National Research Council, immigrants may be adding as much as $10 billion to our economy each year. Indeed, many of the fastest growing corporations in America have been started by immigrants. For example, Intel, Sun Microsystems, Computer Associates, Solectron, and Lam Research are high-tech companies each employing thousands, even tens of thousands, of native-born workers and collectively generating revenues in the billions of dollars.

As the Senate Judiciary Subcommittee on Immigration conducts a series of hearings on immigration policy, however, anxious advocates of nativism have mistakenly convinced many otherwise reasonable Americans that our immigration policies are destroying the social and economic fabric of the nation. The argument plays as well in Boston and San Diego as it does in Peoria: If we eliminate the newcomers, it is said, jobs will be plentiful, the tax burden will decline, and our schools will be vastly improved. What gets totally lost in the heat of the argument, however, is that immigrants are as responsible for job *creation* as they are for job competition. Without the recent influx of foreign investment and skilled labor, our nation might already be headed for permanent stagnation or decline.

Despite this economic reality, too many citizens uncritically accept the stereotypic image of huddled masses of impoverished, uneducated, and disease-ridden refugees from China, Vietnam, Cambodia, and Mexico pounding on the nation's door, ready to steal our jobs and increase our tax burden. Under this assumption, California voters in 1994 passed Proposition 187, the immigration initiative that seeks to cut off most state services to illegal aliens. In 1996, Congress passed a law that allowed for the automatic deportation of legal immigrants who have been convicted of a felony. Also during 1996, Congress came very close to passing legislation that would have severely limited legal immigration. Senator Kennedy was among those who led the fight to defeat these unwarranted, if not dangerous, restrictions.

During the last few years, as income inequality has increased and growing numbers of our citizens have become alarmed about their future economic security, we have heard more and more the charge that immigrants are robbing native-born Americans of their jobs. It doesn't seem to matter that our unemployment rate has dropped to a 24-year low. It is true, of course, that immigrants have long supplied the United States with the cheap labor necessary to an expanding economy. Without newcomers from Latin America, Europe, Asia, and Africa, America would have lacked the manpower to harvest crops, build railroads, and operate the machinery of production.

Moreover, as global competition and automation have taken their toll on the American labor force, immigrants have provided a steady pool of research scientists, teachers, and engineers, enhancing our nation's competitive position in applied science and technology. Under what is known as the Einstein exemption, almost 40% of recent PhDs in physics, mathematics, and engineering are granted to the foreign-born. According to the National Science Foundation, more than two thirds of them remain in the United States after graduation, where they keep America on the scientific and technological cutting edge and prevent even more of our high-tech jobs from relocating to foreign shores.

While Americans continue to complain about having to deal with newcomers, Canadians have done everything possible to encourage wealthy immigrants to invest in their country. Since 1984, more than 110,000 newcomers from Hong Kong alone have settled in one of the Canadian provinces. The result has been to bring jobs, trade, and renewed capitalist spirit to the Canadian economy.

In one of its more rational decisions, Congress passed the Immigration Act of 1990, establishing a status of "investor visas," which permits newcomers who pledge to invest in an economic enterprise that generates or maintains at least 10 jobs in a high unemployment area to enter the United States. However, the minimal investment to obtain these visas—$500,000—is excessive in comparison to the amount required by any other nation. Since 1990, therefore, fewer than 1,000 immigrants have applied for such visas, even though 10,000 per year were allocated by the federal government. By reducing the minimum capital requirements for securing a "green card," the United States would be vastly more effective in competing for the job-creating equity capital now flowing to other countries, especially Canada.

In the midst of hysteria over immigration, Congress may now decide to play the politically expedient "immigration card" by imposing further restrictions that will reduce the flow of foreign investment to a mere trickle. In the process, wealthy immigrants will continue on their way to other nations where they are welcomed with open arms. It is ironic that we are so intent on stopping the newcomers. If we would only permit them, they might create even more jobs for all Americans—even for the most xenophobic among us. ■

# Another Crisis in Black and White?
The Coming Race War in America

The O.J. Simpson verdict was a clarion wake-up call to white America. It was absolutely clear that the majority of black Americans believed Simpson was an innocent victim of racist police officers who conspired to plant incriminating evidence against him. In addition, many blacks similarly believe that nationwide restaurant chains add a secret ingredient to sterilize black men, that soft drink companies are owned by the Ku Klux Klan, and that the U.S. military conspired to infect Africans with AIDS.

After 25 years of teaching and writing about prejudice and violence, I have recently become a prophet of gloom and doom on the issue of race in America, and reactions to the verdict in the Simpson case only serve to reinforce my pessimistic view. Very few white Americans seem ready to acknowledge the intensity of resentment felt by millions of black Americans. While our citizens remain in a state of collective denial, the possibility of a civil war looms large on the national horizon.

Affirmative action may have helped create a viable black middle class, but it hasn't touched the lives of most inner-city blacks. The black underclass is much larger now than it was in the 1960s, when our cities were burning. Some 11 million black Americans continue to live in squalor.

Many black Americans are fed up with being victimized by petty indignities; they are followed around in stores, treated like criminals by the police, and designated intellectually inferior by some white social scientists. As a direct result of the so-called "War Against Drugs," almost 30% of all young black men are presently under the control of the criminal justice system. More than half of all prison inmates are black. Having given up on white society, growing numbers of impoverished blacks have come to embrace the doctrine of "separate but equal" in education and to support the ideology of Afrocentrism.

Race riots in the 1960s never led to a civil war. Thirty years ago, black Americans were indeed angry, but white Americans were not. In evaluating their economic position at the time, whites saw themselves as the beneficiaries of unparalleled prosperity. In the wake of riots across the country, therefore, many whites responded with compassion to what they regarded as a cry for help from the black community.

In sharp contrast to the 1960s, we now live in an age of anger—white Americans are no longer so sympathetic to the problems of people of color, but are concerned instead with their own economic survival. For many whites, the American Dream has become a nightmare. Having been the victims of a massive wave of corporate downsizing in the early 1990s, they feel insecure about their jobs and about maintaining their lifestyles. In the closing years of the century, whites are unlikely to react to rioting with compassion—they are much more likely to respond by fighting fire with fire.

Given the proliferation of firearms in our country, the potential for disaster is exponentially greater now than in the 1960s. There are 250 million handguns on the streets, and semiautomatic assault weapons have become increasingly available. In 30 states, the members of organized militias go into the woods regularly to rehearse for a war they are convinced will be started by the federal government (the enemy).

Revolutions typically occur when a long period of perceived progress is followed by a short period of reversal. In the current cost-cutting atmosphere, black Americans see themselves as bearing the brunt of the economic burden of the nation. Sharp cutbacks in social programs convince black citizens that their problems are being increasingly ignored. In major cities around the country, white-run companies (and therefore jobs) have departed for the suburbs. Foreign competition and automation have eroded the manufacturing jobs that formerly propelled poor people into the working class. As income inequality takes its toll, impoverished blacks feel they have no place to turn except to their guns and their gangs.

The problems of black Americans have been exacerbated as well by the recent influx of Latinos and Asians. Concerns about racism are now being addressed in more inclusive terms. Many blacks regard an interest in diversity or multiculturalism as just another ploy on the part of white Americans seeking to brush aside the difficult problems of racism. There recently have been major confrontations between blacks and newcomers from Asia and Latin America. In a radio interview, a Nation of Islam leader remarked, "Blacks have been in America 437 years, and people who have been here 437 days have walked past us."

Demographers predict a 17% increase in the population of black teenagers over the next decade. Without a profound change in national policy, the most impoverished of these young people will grow up having a general disdain for white America. These are the foot soldiers for black America if it ever comes down to a racial confrontation. They will lack strong national leadership and organization, but they won't need either. The presence of a national media will assure that civil disturbances that begin in one major city spread rapidly to the others. This is precisely how rioting swept across the country in the 1960s.

As a 19-year-old black man recently explained to me with emotion, "You people enslaved us, but we still loved you. You kept us down and we still loved you. But things have changed, and we don't love you anymore. Next time, we will pay you back for the misery you have caused us." ∎

---

### ■ FOCUS  *Suggestions for Further Reading*

"The Economic Escalator" depended a great deal on Kevin Phillips's research in his book *The Politics of the Rich and the Poor* (1990) and Jeffrey Madrick's argument in his book *The End of Affluence* (1995). I also based much of my argument on Katherine Newman's perceptive observations in *Falling From Grace: The Experience of Downward Mobility in the American Middle Class* (1988). As an anthropologist, Newman sees the downwardly mobile as a "very special tribe." She conceives of the experience of generational downward mobility in American society as something "foreign"— a phenomenon as strange to the members of American society as are the exotic rituals in New Guinea.

Some sociologists believe that social inequality is functional and even necessary to the operation of a society. In an early article, "Some Principles of Stratification," in the *American Sociological Review* (1945), Kingsley Davis and Wilbert Moore argue that at least some degree of social stratification is necessary as a means for rewarding the really important positions in a society. In his highly critical response to Davis and Moore, Melvin Tumin later wrote in his *American Sociological Review* article "Some Principles of Stratification: A Critical Analysis" (1953) that institutionalized social inequality was also dysfunctional for society. In other words, stratification has some *negative* consequences that were completely ignored by Davis and Moore. Herbert J. Gans takes a modified version of the functional position when he argues in "The Positive Functions of Poverty," in the *American Journal of Sociology* (1972), that the presence of poverty aids in the survival of a society (for example, poor people get the dirty work done, as we saw earlier in the book).

"An Apple Pie and an Open Mind" suggests that the inspiration for at least some part of the militia movement is economic—many members of the Patriot Movement have suffered financial hardship and are looking for an explanation that makes sense to them. Representing rural poverty, they blame the federal government as well as a host of groups they believe to be in a conspiracy with the federal government to deprive them of their means of livelihood. For an objective account of the rise of the militia movement in the United States, I recommend Jonathan Karl's *The Right to Bear Arms* (1995).

The evidence for "Images of Aging" can be found in a paper titled *Powerful Elders* that I did with Arnold Arluke and William Levin for the 1992 meetings of the American Sociological Association and in *Ageism: Prejudice and Discrimination Against the Elderly* (1980), which Bill Levin and I coauthored. For a summary of the traditional stereotypes associated with older people, see Robert Butler's excellent book, *Why Survive? Being Old in America* (1975). By the way, it was Butler who coined the term *ageism*. A recent book examines the continuance of intergenerational conflict into the new millennium—see Susan MacManus (1996), *Young vs. Old: Generational Combat in the 21st Century*.

Concerning "Immigrants Create Jobs for Americans," I relied a good deal on the numerous journalistic accounts in newspapers and magazines. For a particularly comprehensive analysis of the worldwide movement toward immigration and its implications, see the special edition "World Report" section of the *Los Angeles Times* (October 1, 1991). The modern immigrant experience in America is described and analyzed in *Immigrant America: A Portrait* (1990), by Alejandro Portes and Ruben Rumbaut.

Lewis Coser's safety valve idea suggests that hostility toward immigrants may derive from citizens' dissatisfaction with their economic situation. Rather than direct their anger toward the true source of their deprivations (for example, a president, a ruler, a monarch), they focus their hostility on vulnerable people at the bottom (for example, welfare recipients, underclass members, immigrants). Coser's idea can be found in his classic work *The Functions of Social Conflict* (1956).

In his enlightening book *The Rich Get Richer and the Poor Get Prison* (1989), Jeffrey Reiman presents a criminal justice version of the safety valve function, based on a conflict approach. Reiman attempts to explain why the criminal justice system seems to be preoccupied with dangers usually threatened by violent offenders who are poor. He argues that our attention is diverted from the real source of crime, from the injustices of our economic system, and from those rich and powerful members of society who benefit most from the maintenance of the status quo. The dangerous activities of the rich are rarely defined by the legal system as crimes, he says, although such activities result in hundreds of thousands of deaths and the loss of billions of dollars. But the wealthy are weeded out at every stage of the criminal justice system. And in the failure of the criminal justice system, there is a victory for the rich: Hostility is redirected away from the top of the economic order and focused instead on the poor people in our society.

Regarding "Another Crisis in Black and White?" Carl T. Rowan's book *The Coming Race War in America* (1996) was published some 12 months after my column suggesting a similar scenario was printed in the *Boston Globe*. For an excellent analysis of how inequality has actually affected the black underclass, read William J. Wilson's *The Truly Disadvantaged* (1987). He argues that the growing problem of permanent poverty among young black men in urban areas can be traced not to any intellectual deficit but to the movement of jobs to the suburbs and to the trend toward a postindustrial economy. Melvin L. Oliver and Thomas M. Shapiro's award-winning book *Black Wealth/White Wealth* argues persuasively that racial inequality has had a much greater impact than is suggested by differences in income. Oliver and Shapiro demonstrate that racial differences in private wealth—assets and debt—leave black Americans in a profoundly disadvantaged position. ∎

■ **DEVELOPING IDEAS** *About Social Inequality*

1. Research topic: Make a list of 20 occupations representing the kinds of jobs that you and your classmates are likely to be doing after graduation. Give this list to several friends and ask them to rank all 20 occupations from 1 (most prestigious) to 20 (least prestigious). How much agreement is there regarding the prestige rankings of these jobs? What do your results indicate about the *structured* aspect of stratification?

2. Writing topic: Write a short essay in which you compare the everyday lives of two fictitious characters: a 25-year-old man who possesses extraordinary wealth versus a 25-year-old man who experiences extreme poverty. Specifically, compare them on such things as (a) what they are likely to do at leisure, (b) where they are likely to live, (c) their family lives, (d) health care, and (e) their jobs. Explain how each man—the wealthy and the poor—got that way and what the poverty-stricken man might do to improve his social position.

3. Research topic: Popular culture often expresses our stereotyped images. Analyze any 10 birthday cards that you select from your local card shop or drug store. Choose only cards that make a direct reference to age. Are their messages—aside from Happy Birthday—positive or negative? How many refer, if *only* in a joking reference, to lack of sexual activity, lack of attractiveness, lack of intelligence, lack of physical ability? How many joke about age concealment? How many make special mention of women's problems with aging? Does any card suggest that you might get better as you get older?

4. Writing topic: Make a list of all the tasks that poor people do for society—tasks that might otherwise not get done or might have to be done by middle-class types. For example, poor people buy day-old bread from thrift stores that might otherwise never be sold. Your turn. By the way, can you also suggest *other ways* to get these tasks accomplished without relying on poor people to do them?

5. Research topic: Among the methods that sociologists use for assessing social status is the subjective approach, whereby the respondents are asked to place themselves in the stratification hierarchy. In 1949, Richard Centers asked a national sample of white adults, "If you were asked to use one of these four names

for your social class, which would you say you belonged in: the middle class, the lower class, working class, or upper class?" Like many other sociologists, Centers found that the majority of his sample saw themselves as belonging to the middle class. Using the same question as Centers, take a sample of 20 people you know fairly well and determine how they see their social class membership—as upper, middle, working, or lower? With which class does the majority identify? Explain your results.

6. Research topic: Every year, the U.S. Bureau of the Census produces a volume, easily accessible at most libraries or through the U.S. Government Printing Office, entitled *Statistical Abstract of the United States.* To determine how inequality may have increased or decreased over time, compare at least 2 years (say, 1 year from the 1990s vs. 1 year from the 1970s) on several indicators of economic well-being such as unemployment rate, total personal income, families below the poverty level, and average annual pay. You can find these indicators in the table of contents of the book in sections on "Labor Force, Employment, and Earnings" and "Income, Expenditures, and Wealth." You may also decide to look in the section on "Business Enterprise" for business failure rate and employment growth by major industry. It might be interesting, in addition, to compare two groups—say, blacks and whites—on the same indicators of economic well-being over time. ■

# PART SEVEN

## Social Change

Nothin' lasts. And nothing stays the same. What was once the quiet country lane of our youth becomes the whirling interstate of today. Whereas social change affects every aspect of our social life, it also has a real impact on our environment and material goods.

L ast time I went on a diet, it took me 3 months to lose 24 pounds. Twenty years ago, it would have been relatively easy for me to lose 34 pounds over a short period of time. I would simply have cut down a little on sweets and also reduced the quantity of what I ate at meals. Now that I have reached middle age, however, losing weight seems to require more than just a minor adjustment in my diet. It's not that I lack the will; it's that my metabolism has changed over the years. As a result, only a severe drop in calorie intake along with some kind of exercise regimen seems to make any difference. I really understand, on a gut level, why so many Americans suffer from middle-age spread. If you ask me, the more you age, the more you must reduce your intake of calories to maintain the same weight. Medical research supports my belief.

Just as the structure and functioning of the human body are modified with age, so, too, the structure of our social lives is capable of profound change. In a sense, the "metabolism" of our society changes over time. More and more women have entered the labor force, 25% of all college students are now over 30, and the homicide rate has fallen. It was inconceivable, just a few years ago, that the Berlin Wall would come down or that the Soviet Union would crumble, and yet these changes are now taken-for-granted realities.

By *social change*, then, we refer to modifications in either culture or social structure. Interestingly enough, much social change is orderly. Just as structure has discernible characteristics, so change often has patterns.

Theorists disagree as to precisely what that social change looks like. In the 19th century, theorists such as Herbert Spencer argued that societies inevitably *evolve* from the simple to the complex and always toward greater and greater progress. Karl Marx suggested instead that societies develop through a series of definite stages—from primitive communism, feudalism, capitalism, to socialism—depending on the organization of their economic institutions. Marx believed that all history is the history of class conflict. Finally, some sociologists saw a cyclical pattern in social change. They asserted that history repeats itself. Pitirim Sorokin, for example, identified three cultural themes—ideational, sensate, and idealistic—through which the pendulum of change swings back and forth.

This brief summary of social change theory is meant only to indicate its diversity. Most modern-day sociologists would agree that the earlier theories of social change were too simple. Spencer's views need to be modified: Not all change is for the better; some is for the worse. Progress is far from inevitable. Marx's views need to be modified: Not all conflict is class based. In modern life, we see conflicts between political alliances, age groups, countries, religions, racial groups, and so on. Many of these conflicts generate social change. Sorokin's views need to be modified: The pendulum of change doesn't necessarily swing on the course that he predicted.

Still, the idea of evolution continues to play an important role in our thinking about social change. There seems to be a strong tendency for culture and social structure to become more complex over time. Societies tend to move from small-scale and simple to large-scale and complex forms. Unlike living organisms, however, the evolution cannot be characterized as inevitable. Moreover, the direction and speed of change are not the same in all societies. Societies seem to evolve but on their own terms.

On an individual level, there are literally millions of people who go on diets and take up exercise programs to influence the course of biological change. Many avoid fatty foods, cut down on sugar, or give up red meat. Others buy treadmills and exercise bicycles or jog on a daily basis. Such efforts don't always work as well as we would like. In fact, some dieting plans have an incredibly high 90% failure rate over the long term.

Human beings have similarly sought to help social change along in one or another area of concern. Since 1960, for example, we have seen numerous programs and policies directed toward improving public education; reducing racial, age, and gender discrimination; combating violent crime; improving the economy; and aiding the mentally ill. As suggested in "The Boomerang Effect," not all of these efforts have succeeded as planned. In fact, some of them have only backfired by creating even more social problems for us to solve. The failure rate of programs and policies may not approach 90%, but our effectiveness could be better.

In the 1940s, sociologist Robert Merton recognized that unanticipated and anomalous results—perhaps even the boomerang effect—are rather commonplace in sociological research. Such unexpected, even surprising findings may not always generate the most effective proposals for change at the time, but they frequently have a positive consequence as well. In being forced to deal with inconsistencies and contradictions, sociologists must rethink their work, extend their inadequate theories, or create new theories that better explain the phenomena they seek to understand. In the long run, their *serendipitous* findings may become the basis for more powerful theories of social behavior and more effective social policies and planning.

One thing that I learned the hard way about dieting is that timing is everything. If you're not ready to make the commitment, don't bother trying. If you can't dedicate yourself to an exercise regimen, don't make the effort. You will only fail.

In "Fads: Is Goldfish Gobbling Next?" we observe that popular fads and fashions since the 1920s have depended on the "timing" of changes in the larger culture. Indeed, many fads are made possible by large-scale cultural change. For example, our shared ideas regarding sexuality had been modified so much during the 1960s "sexual revolution" that "streaking" became a widespread activity on college campuses and was usually considered a harmless prank or minor annoyance. Ten years earlier, however, the same act of public nudity would probably have been regarded as a major sexual perversion, and offenders would have been immediately shuffled off to serve long sentences in prison or in a mental hospital.

The aging of the human body is a "mixed bag" of developmental changes. For many people, advanced aging brings about an increase in verbal ability, a more mellow temperament, and more of a tendency to vote. But aging can also engender problems, such as a worsening of both memory and hearing.

A major theme in "Riding the Rumor Mill" is that long-standing rumors about crime and disaster in suburban shopping malls actually mirror a trend in the "aging" of our society that many Americans view with alarm. Those social problems once associated with the "inner city" are now spreading to the suburbs, formerly regarded as bastions of middle-class respectability. Suburbanites often express anxiety about maintaining their lifestyle by contributing to unfounded rumors of the demise of the shopping mall. Though focusing on the safety of the mall, they actually express anxiety about more basic changes in their lives.

The human body is a system of interrelated parts. A change in one area has implications for other areas as well. Thus, a healthy diet and sensible exercise program will likely strengthen the functioning of the heart, kidneys, and lungs.

The parts of our society similarly affect one another. "Highway to Hell?" examines the effect of an item of American material culture called the automobile on everyday forms of behavior. Anyone who routinely commutes in rush hour traffic knows the meaning of the term "hot under the collar." Unfortunately, the presence of thousands of pounds of steel in the control of angry and frustrated commuters helps to create the conditions necessary for violent outbursts. Even worse, some motorists who are already angry before they get on the highway decide to go for a drive to "cool off." This creates an explosive mix. Keep in mind, "Highway to Hell?" focuses our attention not on the personality characteristics of drivers but directly on a social situation—the act of driving on our roadways—as it influences differing conceptions of deviant behavior over the decades. But there is another important sociological issue to address: Exactly why did the automobile have such a profound influence on the shape of American cities? And why didn't Americans maximize the use of public transportation?

Of course, it's not just the automobile that represents systematic changes over time. Change the structure of the American family (for example, by increasing the number of dual-career families) and you change the economy as well. Change our political institutions and you change the character of mass communication. Thus, "Enquiring Times" isn't only about newspapers and books. You don't have to read between the lines to see that celebrity gossip has become an important force in politics and mass entertainment. In the presidential campaign of 1988, for example, Gary Hart was a target; in the more recent election campaign, it was Bill Clinton. Gossip was very much involved in the televised senate hearings to confirm Justice Clarence Thomas and in the televised rape trial of William Kennedy Smith. Millions of Americans "eavesdropped" on an entire cast of characters—Thomas, Hill, Smith—as they divulged the intricate details of their private lives. More recently, O. J. Simpson and the deaths of Nicole Brown Simpson and Ronald Goldman provided the focal point for small talk during prime time. Then, just when we seemed to be experiencing a gossip lull, it turned out to be the lull before the gossip storm—President Clinton with Paula Jones and Monica Lewinsky. Some cultures will cut off your lips for gossiping. Here, we just put it on national TV! ∎

# The Boomerang Effect in Planning Social Change
In the Social Arena, Good Intentions Sometimes Go Wrong

Usually, social policies and programs are a "mixed bag"; they have multiple effects. We should have learned this lesson from our experience with "hard scientists," who have long recognized the need to weigh costs against benefits in evaluating outcomes. Thalidomide probably eased the suffering of numerous pregnant women; unfortunately, it also produced serious birth deformities. Urea formaldehyde made an extremely effective form of home insulation; it also made some people sick. Antipsychotic drugs improve everyday psychological functioning, but when prescribed without caution, they can also produce an irreversible nervous disorder.

In the social arena, affirmative action legislation has opened doors for women and minorities who would otherwise have been summarily excluded from many decent jobs. It has also stigmatized its beneficiaries by giving the impression that blacks, Latinos, and women enjoy an unfair advantage and are not qualified for the jobs that they hold. Similarly, Social Security is, for many older people, the difference between survival and starvation; it also leads millions of young people to believe that they have no choice but to retire by the age of 65 or 70.

Aside from government intervention, multiple effects often confound those who give the rest of us advice. Marriage counselors who encourage troubled couples to "air their differences" may make their clients feel more comfortable with themselves; they may also inadvertently precipitate a divorce by escalating conflicts between husbands and wives. Nursing homes frequently provide humane care; they also foster dependence. And the voluntary rating system used by the motion picture industry provides guidance in the selection of movies appropriate for children; it also stimulates countless cinematic scenes of gratuitous sex and violence to justify a PG or R rating (the G rating is the kiss of death for the commercial success of a film).

The same principle applies to the influence of the generations. To their credit, people who grew up in the 1960s were deeply involved in the civil rights and women's movements. But they must also take the blame for having weakened our resolve to teach basic skills to our youngsters. We demolished the unstructured classroom later because we realized we were producing a generation of well-adjusted functional illiterates.

In some cases, intelligent people implementing intelligent policies are responsible for producing a "boomerang effect"; they actually create more of whatever it is they seek to reduce in the first place. The boomerang effect has been achieved many times in recent years by men and women of good will. State legislatures around the nation have recently raised the drinking age back to 21 in an effort to reduce the prevalence of violent deaths among our young people. But such policies seem instead to have created the conditions for even more campus violence. Some college students who previously drank in bars and lounges under the watchful supervision of bouncers (not to mention owners eager to keep their liquor licenses) now retreat to the sanctuary of their fraternity houses and apartments, where they no longer control their behavior—or their drinking.

The boomerang effect has also played a role in attempts to reduce the availability of illicit drugs. During the 1980s, the federal government was quite successful in reducing the supply of, albeit not the demand for, street drugs such as marijuana. As fields burned and contraband was confiscated, the price of marijuana skyrocketed to a point where cheap alternatives (for example, crack cocaine) began to compete in the marketplace. Unfortunately, the cheap alternatives were even more harmful than the illicit drugs they replaced. In addition, crack wars between competing dealers for territory and markets were responsible for escalating the violence on our city streets. Our official response was to fill our prisons to capacity with street-level dealers and addicts. Meanwhile, teenaged drug use only soared out of sight.

One final area should be mentioned in connection with the boomerang effect. Every state has now established a system of registering those ex-offenders who have committed sex crimes against minors. At the national level, moreover, Congress recently enacted legislation that creates a national registry to track released sex offenders when they move from state to state. Establishing a database for the purpose of informing the local police or the FBI of a sex offender's presence may, of course, be useful for identifying potential suspects when a sex crime occurs. But notifying the neighbors that an ex-offender is in their community only assures that he will be shoved out of mainstream society and pushed into a life of crime. As soon as the word gets around, he undoubtedly will lose his job, be evicted from his apartment, and be shunned by his friends and neighbors. He may even become a victim of violence perpetrated by anxious parents. Then, he will move to someone else's city or town, only to be humiliated and rejected again. No wonder that so many ex-offenders have chosen to defy the law and not to register at all, though they face arrest and prosecution. Rather than make it possible by law to inform the neighbors, we should really get tough on dangerous sex offenders. Let's make certain that they never get into our neighborhoods in the first place—not unless they are ready to behave themselves.

Lest those who argue for a "hands-off policy" get too smug, I suggest that the failure to act also has its unanticipated side effects. Ronald Reagan's "benign neglect" in response to poverty in America during the 1980s may have helped cut double-digit inflation; it also reduced the size of the middle class and increased permanent poverty in our cities to an unprecedented level. Moreover, in what was euphemistically called "deinstitutionalization," we emptied our nation's mental hospitals in the 1970s without providing adequate services or supervision for the mentally ill individuals released into the community. Some of them joined the growing ranks of the homeless; many stopped taking the medications that had made possible their release from institutions.

Of course, not all policies are as well-intentioned as they may appear to be. How do we ascertain another person's motives, let alone those of an organization? Was the ratings system initiated to help parents or to get government off the back of the movie industry? Did all those who supported emptying our mental hospitals really desire more humane treatment of the mentally ill, or were they merely trying to cut costs? Even motivation is often a mixed bag.

If a spokesperson for the cigarette industry claims that the link between smoking and lung cancer has not been established, we are suspicious. We may perceive a self-serving, biased assessment. Exactly the same skeptical mind-set is valuable in evaluating the effectiveness of social services and policies—skepticism without cynicism. ■

# Fads
## Is Goldfish Gobbling Next?

With the all-purpose response "I know, Mom, but everyone's doing it," millions of teenagers have sought to explain to their parents why they experiment with drugs or alcohol, color their hair purple, or wear multiple pierced earrings. Their desire to conform to fashions of their fellows is more than an excuse. Adolescents often do what everyone else is doing; they go along with a fad or fashion simply because they don't want to look different or to be seen as out of step with their peers. Given their other-directedness, teenagers are especially sensitive to what is current versus passé, what is "in" versus "out."

It should come as no surprise, therefore, that many fads and fashions originate in what is called adolescent subculture. By conforming to the latest crazes in haircuts, dress, music, and gadgetry, many teenagers hope to gain approval from their friends.

But peer approval is not the only appeal of such fads. While they hope to impress their friends with their compliance, teenagers also seek to distance themselves from their parents. As a result, behavior that appears to adults to be irrational and even dysfunctional may be valued by the young for exactly that reason: Such behavior is outrageous to the older generation. If, when young, their parents drank beer, then the teenagers will try marijuana; if parents wore long hair and love beads, their offspring will shave their initials into their hair or don spiked jewelry or join the Young Republicans; if parents wore their designer labels under their garments, then their offspring will insist on wearing their labels outside.

Ironically, and of course unwittingly, even the most outrageous teenage fads touchingly reflect the tenor of their times. During the Roaring Twenties, for example, Charles Lindbergh and Amelia Earhart were busy setting records with their derring-do across the Atlantic. Rapid industrial growth and expanding capitalism generated intense competition for scarce economic resources. How did the "flaming youth" of the decade respond? With contests of skill and endurance: flagpole sitting, rocking chair derbies, cross-country races, pea-eating contests, kissing and dancing marathons, gum-chewing and peanut-pushing contests.

During the Sputnik era of the late 1950s, competition was once again intense. The United States and the Soviet Union vied for supremacy in science and technology, and American schools responded by attempting to raise their standards. Teenagers once more designed contests to set and break records. Throughout the decade, young people crammed themselves into hearses, Volkswagen Beetles, and telephone booths. They stacked dozens of students on a single bed and stuffed their rooms with papers.

Teenage fashion has also been affected by the culture of its period. During the 1920s, when American women were first allowed to vote, youthful "flappers" literally threw off the corsets of their mother's generation in favor of knee-length (short) skirts, shapeless gowns, and bobbed hair. Some 40 years later, motivated by the women's movement of the 1960s, teenage girls wore miniskirts and burned their bras.

Conventional values influence adolescent fads in yet another way. They set the limits as to just how far those fads are permitted to go before adult society enforces sanctions against them. In 1974, undergraduates began to engage in "streaking." To streak was to dash nude through a public place.

Society's tolerance for streaking was a result of the sexual revolution of the 1960s. The same act would undoubtedly have received quite a different reception if it had occurred during the 1950s. Any student who had dared run naked through a college campus then would, in all likelihood, have been quickly locked away as a sexual pervert and a menace to society. In 1954, streaking could hardly have gained the popularity of a fad.

Even the most absurd practices can become the basis for an adolescent fad, given the right social climate. During the Great Depression of the 1930s, at a time when many Americans were having trouble putting food on the table, parents lost their appetites because of a fad that hit college campuses. From Massachusetts to Missouri, students had taken to swallowing goldfish.

A Harvard freshman was the first to swallow a single live fish, while fellow students at the Freshman Union looked on in disgust. Three weeks later, an undergraduate at Franklin and Marshall in Lancaster, Pennsylvania, ate 3 goldfish.

New records for goldfish consumption were then set almost daily. At the University of Pennsylvania, one intrepid soul swallowed 25; at the University of Michigan, 28; at Boston College, 29; at Northeastern University, 38; at MIT, 42; and at Clark University, 89 were devoured at one sitting. One college student gained fame by coming up with the first recipe for a goldfish sugar cookie; the chef at the Hotel Statler put the dish on the menu as a special. But a pathologist with the U.S. Public Health Service cautioned that goldfish could contain tapeworms that might lodge in the intestines and cause anemia, and by the spring of 1939, the goldfish-gobbling craze had gone the way of the dance marathon.

Teenagers in 1990 tripped over their own feet by wearing their sneakers unlaced; to this day, they continue to increase their susceptibility to illness by refusing to wear winter hats or raincoats and ruin their feet with pointed-toe shoes, all because the refusal to wear these things is in fashion. In general, they are seen as doing things that aren't very good for them—tattooing their bodies, piercing their tongues, noses, and navels, engaging in so-called extreme sports like snowboarding, and listening to Marilyn Manson. Most teenagers aren't swallowing goldfish yet, but for those who are too young to remember, that could very well be next. ∎

# Riding the Rumor Mill
Our Basic Anxieties Are Projected in Various Tall Tales

Rumors frequently touch on our important fears and anxieties. Where food shortages exist, individuals circulate stories about the supply and distribution of provisions; where access to economic resources depends on tracing descent through uncertain genealogies, they gossip about one another's ancestors; where witchcraft is a cultural belief, they spread tales about who is and is not a witch; and when economic times are bad, workers depend on the office grapevine to forecast management changes.

Temple University's Ralph Rosnow suggests that rumors on a national level prey on our basic anxieties about death, disaster, and illness. Thus, a number of celebrities have reportedly died in the face of overwhelming evidence to the contrary (including their personal denials)—Paul McCartney, Jerry Mathers of *Leave It to Beaver* fame, and Life Cereal's "Mikey," to mention a few. Some who have, by all credible accounts, actually died—Elvis, Jim Morrison, JFK, Selena, and Hitler—have been seen alive! In addition, many rumors have incorrectly reported the contamination of popular food; for example, spider eggs in bubble gum, candy that explodes when eaten with a carbonated beverage, worms in hamburgers, mice in Coke bottles, rats in fried chicken, and cats in Chinese food.

Most of the time, it is impossible to track a rumor to its original source. Once in a while, however, a rumor can be traced. In 1998, for example, a medical researcher tried to extort millions of dollars from a fast-food hamburger company by claiming that he had found a french-fried tail in his son's meal. The researcher was convicted of fraud by a federal jury, after it was learned that he had placed the rat tail in his son's french fries.

According to Tulane sociologist Fredrick Koenig, author of *Rumor in the Marketplace: The Social Psychology of Commercial Hearsay*, rumors do not necessarily reduce anxiety; instead, they often confirm our worst suspicions. But in one sense, such doomsday stories can also be comforting, for at the very least, they confirm the validity of our perception of the world, especially if we see that world as dangerous.

The anxiety multiplies when the "danger" is seen as encroaching on our personal safety. Take living in the suburbs, for example. For decades, young families scrimped and sacrificed, denying themselves all but the barest necessities to accumulate the down payment on their "dream house" in East Norwich, New York; Longmeadow, Massachusetts; or Glencoe, Illinois. By moving to the suburbs, they had hoped to escape the poverty, crime, and congestion associated with city living.

But during the past decade or two, the suburban version of the American Dream slipped away, as real estate values and property taxes skyrocketed, the quality of local services declined, pollution increased, energy costs remained high, and crime invaded the outer reaches of suburbia. On a daily basis, local newspapers reported increasing incidents of the very crimes that anxious suburbanites had left the city to escape—forcible rape, aggravated assault, and automobile theft. Facing severe tax restrictions at the local level, suburban school systems began laying off teachers, firemen, and police. Public roads and buildings were left in a state of disrepair. And in the process, the suburbs increasingly began to assume the pathologies associated with urban decay.

In 1979, tension surrounding an "invader" of the suburbs, Reverend Sun Myung Moon's Unification Church, the so-called Moonies, which purchased real estate in Gloucester, Massachusetts, manifested in a "classic" rumor. Hearing stories of teenagers coerced into the Moonie cause, people began believing that the regionally powerful Entenmann's Bakery was owned by the Unification Church and that its products were tainted.

Although Entenmann's was then actually owned by the Warner-Lambert Corporation, that detail didn't stop hundreds of customers from complaining to store managers who carried Entenmann's products. Moreover, church bulletins, letters to the editor, and callers to radio talk shows all warned about Moonie ownership of the bakery and urged everyone to boycott Entenmann's products. As they attempted to deliver their goods, Entenmann's drivers were physically assaulted by angry customers. The bakery's sales declined. So long as public anxiety remained at a high level, Entenmann's continued to serve as a convenient, albeit innocent, target of hostility.

Eventually, the anxieties fueling the Entenmann's rumors faded into the distance. In its place, rumormongering about the deterioration of suburbia coalesced around images of the shopping mall as dangerous and threatening, as a place where the most pernicious influences of the inner city had altered suburban life. After all, the mall had previously represented the heart and soul of the suburban lifestyle, being almost inaccessible except by automobile, protected from crime by security guards, sheltered by its physical isolation, and attractive to a largely homogeneous segment of the middle-class customers who spent their days leisurely strolling through the corridors spending money. If crime and poverty invaded the tranquil, secure confines of the suburban shopping mall, then absolutely nobody was safe.

In 1983, in western Massachusetts, there surfaced a story about a "woman" shopping at a local mall who asked various customers for a ride home. It was said that when authorities finally apprehended her, she turned out to be an axe-wielding man wearing makeup and a wig to protect his true identity. Similarly in the early 1980s, Connecticut residents picked up various stories about a young girl who suddenly disappeared while walking with her mother in a mall. According to this tale, worried security guards later found her in a restroom, where she had been given a short haircut and dressed in boy's clothing. By 1985, some version of these mall stories had spread all over the country from New York to Texas to California. Only the name of the shopping center and some of the details of the crime varied from location to location.

The rumors of abduction and crime in suburban shopping malls, although not completely gone, have receded somewhat. But in their place, there are new reports around the country that newly constructed shopping malls are in imminent danger of being transformed into underground shopping centers; they are, it is said, structurally unsound and literally sinking.

In the most recent episode, the mammoth, three-story Emerald Square Mall in North Attleboro, Massachusetts has been the target of unfounded rumors since it opened in August 1989. Among the most widely told tales are those that contend that the mall has already sunk 6 inches, that its third floor has been closed, that the top floor of the adjoining parking garage has been closed, that the garage has separated from the main building, that many of the windows have shattered, that the mall will soon close, and that the mall will be torn down and rebuilt. Although there is no truth in any of this, that hasn't prevented customers from phoning the mall's building inspector with wild stories, excitedly discussing the rumors in shops and restaurants, and, in some cases, taking their business elsewhere.

Those who attempt to explain such rumors of sinking shopping malls might point to some offhand, ill-informed remark made by an engineer or the presence of a neighboring shopping center that really did have structural problems. People sometimes do get confused by the facts. But for those who take a long-term view, the sinking-mall rumors are merely a new variation of an old theme, beginning with the stories of children allegedly being abducted from mall restrooms and continuing with the axe-wielding "woman." You don't have to be Freud to figure it out: It really isn't the shopping mall sinking we worry about—it is our whole way of life. ∎

# Highway to Hell?
Fear and Loathing on the Road

Travel any highway into a major city during rush hour. While waiting to move, you are bound to observe at least a half dozen drivers talking to themselves, singing along with a tune on the radio, or scratching themselves.

Automobiles give an *illusion* of privacy. So long as drivers remain behind the wheel, they travel in isolation. Enclosed by steel and glass, they are physically independent of the thousands of other motorists with whom they share the road. No matter how jammed the highway is with vehicles, drivers feel alone, and in a social-psychological sense, they are. As a result, they may engage in bizarre, even deviant, behavior.

Having been associated with deviance ever since the advent of mass motoring, automobiles have long contributed to the direction of social and cultural change. In the 1920s, many Americans for the first time owned a family car. And it was the automobile that critics blamed for what they saw as a precipitous decline in national morality. Newly freed from the rigid restrictions of previous generations, the "flaming youth" of the decade regarded the family's "Tin Lizzie" as their "apartment on wheels"—a place where they could kiss, neck, and pet. Sex researcher Alfred Kinsey reported that young women of the 1920s were far more likely to have premarital intercourse than were those who had reached sexual maturity before World War I. Not surprisingly, the automobile was blamed—and with cause. In Robert and Helen Lynd's 1929 classic community study *Middletown*, the overwhelming majority of teenagers in Muncie, Indiana, reported that the automobile was the most common place to pet.

In a more extreme version of immorality, the automobile of the 1920s also became a "brothel on wheels," providing ladies of the night from red light districts around the country a secure and secluded place where they might escape police oversight and ply their trade. The use of the automobile for purposes of prostitution posed a serious setback to the vigorous antivice campaigns of the World War I period. The police were not yet equipped to patrol city streets and country highways.

By the 1950s, teenagers around the country were holding their "submarine races" in lovers' lanes and drive-in theaters. The game of "chicken" became a deadly contest between males who sought to impress their dates. During subsequent decades, young people relied on their automobiles as a safe haven in which to drink beer, have sex, and smoke dope.

Teenagers aren't the only drivers who play chicken. Every year, some 46,000 Americans from all age groups are killed in motor vehicle accidents. Another 1.8 million are disabled. Among the leading causes of such fatal crashes are drinking and speeding—two human factors that could be totally controlled. In some single-victim automobile "accidents," the lack of control is deliberate: The driver purposely veers into a tree or off a bridge to commit suicide. These victims choose an automobile as an instrument for taking their own lives to save their families the embarrassment that accompanies more obvious forms of suicide.

But most deaths and injuries are avoidable. Such accidents happen because the automobile offers power—especially to the powerless. The automobile is a vehicle that satisfies the desire to be in charge. Even the most timid and passive individuals (or perhaps *especially* the most timid and passive individuals) may become fearless bullies and criminals as soon as they get behind the 3,000 pounds of steel that separate them from the rest of humanity. Not only do they feel anonymous; they also feel invulnerable—caught up in an *illusion* of their own omnipotence.

At the extreme, unbridled power turns nasty, and arguments between drivers erupt into violence. The freeways of California have been particularly violent for the past decade or so, as small provocations send some frustrated motorists into a state of frenzy. In Sacramento, a passenger inflamed by a freeway lane change lifted a rifle from a rack in the back window of his pickup truck and fatally shot the driver of the other vehicle. One passenger was shot in the head after a minor sideswiping incident. A tow truck operator was fired on by a driver who had blocked his entry onto the Golden State Freeway. In Claremont, the windshields of 10 vehicles were smashed and a police officer was fired on as he prepared to write a traffic ticket. During a single 2-week period in August, there were 18 different acts of violence on the highways of the Silicon Valley, and this does not include those acts of violence perpetrated in the rest of California. What is more, shooting episodes quickly spread across the country to trigger-happy drivers in Detroit, Boston, and New York.

For commuters, the experience of driving in rush hour traffic is intensely frustrating. In most major cities, parking places have become as rare as pollution-free air, and traffic jams at 5 p.m. are beginning to resemble never-ending parking lots. For visitors, the problems associated with negotiating traffic are exacerbated by a lack of street signs and the presence of one-way streets without pattern or logic. Then, there is the growing *density* of traffic—the number of miles driven increased 35% between 1988 and 1997—but, over the same period of time, only 1% more roads were constructed.

No wonder that 80% of all drivers are now angry most or all of the time, at least according to a 1997 survey conducted by a Michigan firm, EPIC-MRA. Moreover, some drivers are already frustrated and angry before they get behind the wheel of their vehicles. They decide to go for a drive to "cool off" after arguing with their boss, their spouse, or their friends. According to University of California psychologist Joseph Tupin, people with aggressive impulses frequently take their cars out for a spin as a release from the tensions of the day. They get into a minor confrontation on the highway and explode.

Of course, the most pervasive effects of the automobile are at the level of social change. As we have seen, the presence of the family car, beginning in the 1920s, significantly altered the ability of young people to achieve independence from their families. At the same time, the opportunities for deviant behavior became much more difficult to challenge. Moreover, the pattern of commuting traffic in most major cities has determined, for the most part, the clustering of skyscrapers, the placement of sports arenas and convention centers, the direction of suburban sprawl, and the aesthetics of urban life generally. In a few cities (for example, Los Angeles), the urban landscape is virtually dominated by the presence of interconnected networks of freeways.

Americans continue their love affair with their cars. No matter how efficient, public transportation will probably never quite take the place of the beloved automobile. After all, the gargantuan automobile industry (not to mention all of the peripheral industries that it has spawned) literally cannot afford for that to happen and so continues to spend incredibly large amounts of money for advertisements and commercials in which the virtues of driving are extolled. It is perhaps no exaggeration to suggest that the automobile is now as American as apple pie. Of course, so is violence. ∎

# Enquiring Times
## The Tabloidization of Hard News

I confess to having thumbed through a copy or two of the *National Enquirer* and the *Star*, usually while waiting in line at the supermarket checkout counter. It takes little more than a cursory reading to discover that the "two-headed baby" stories—the gory items for which they are notorious—have all but disappeared. According to an article in *Journalism Quarterly*, the tabloids now print profiles: 61% of their articles focus on celebrities (singer Michael Jackson's obsession with cleanliness, Dolly Parton's diet, Burt Reynolds' romantic relationships) and 37% on the accomplishments of ordinary people who do extraordinary things (the man who lost 350 pounds by stapling his stomach, the 87-year-old woman who gave up her Social Security check to feed the homeless, the man who swam for 4 days in shark-infested waters).

For those who prefer the gore, there are still a few, relatively obscure tabloids that specialize in it. The *Sun* and the *Weekly World News* can be counted on for a story featuring "human pregnant with animal" or "animal pregnant with human." But the most popular supermarket tabloids—the *National Enquirer*, the *Star*, the *Globe*, and the *National Examiner*—have removed most of the grisly pieces, and they still attract some 10 million readers.

These tabloids continue to run into thorny ethical problems, however, mainly concerning their aggressive methods of reporting and their reliance on hearsay rather than "hard news." Hollywood celebrities often claim that *Enquirer* reporters invade their privacy, rely on unreliable informants, and fabricate information about their personal lives. Some continue to believe that overly aggressive tabloid paparazzi following Princess Diana's automobile contributed to the crash that killed her. As a result, tabloids continue to have only marginal status among print journalists.

Yet mainstream journalists must be aware, perhaps even envious, of the tremendous popularity of supermarket tabloids. At a time when newspapers around the country are shutting down, publishers are looking for new models that might keep them in business.

Because of their vast appeal, the supermarket tabloids have provided such a model. Many mainstream papers have become *tabloidized;* that is, they have imitated not only the tabloid's size and shape but its sensational headlines. Some have begun to rely more on hearsay and ethically questionable investigative techniques. The *National Enquirer* continues to be the butt of criticism from Hollywood celebrity types, television talk show hosts, and the public. It remains a whipping boy of mainstream journalists, even as they imitate its content and format.

Before we blame the messenger for sending a message we detest, let us recognize that the tabloidization of news reflects a large-scale social change: Gossip about powerful people has assumed an important place in the American psyche. During the 1960s, we treated our rich and famous like royalty. They could do no wrong—and if they did, we would look the other way. John F. Kennedy's acts of infidelity in the White House were well known yet summarily ignored by the press. Whatever their faults and frailties, the rich and powerful were still regarded as paragons of virtue and exemplars for the ethical and intellectual standards we hoped to impart to our children. Nobody wanted to make our heroes into monsters.

In the wake of Watergate, Chappaquiddick, Abscam, Irangate, Jim and Tammy Bakker, Leona Helmsley, Ivan Boesky, Whitewater, Bob Packwood, Paula Jones, and the savings and loan scandal, however, public naïveté gave way to widespread skepticism, if not outright cynicism. We could no longer trust the people who ran things—the national politicians, Hollywood celebrities, and New York business tycoons. They were caught too often literally with their pants down.

In response to an apparently insatiable appetite for gossip, information about the private lives of public figures has become a mainstay of front-page news, just as it has long been the backbone of tabloid journalism. It was not the *Star* or the *National Examiner* but the legitimate *Las Vegas Sun* that first revealed that Liberace was dying of AIDS. It was not the *National Examiner* but the *Miami Herald* that snooped on Gary Hart to expose his affair with Donna Rice. Gossip about the lives of such celebrities as Bill Clinton, Kitty Dukakis, Nancy Reagan, Barney Frank, Ted Kennedy, Martin Luther King, Jr., and Gerry Studds has been featured in front-page stories, not only in the *Star* but in local newspapers around the country. Gossip about Bill Clinton's womanizing was featured not only in mainstream newspapers and magazines such as *Newsweek* but also on network newscasts and web sites. Indeed, during the first days of allegations concerning Clinton's affair with a 21-year-old White House intern, his press secretary's news conference was considered important enough by TV producers that it preempted regularly scheduled programs.

Some people still remember Carol Burnett's successful mid-1970s lawsuit against the *National Enquirer*. She was able to show that the tabloid had acted with reckless disregard for the truth when it published defamatory information about her. According to University of Arkansas Law Professor Rodney Smolla, the establishment press tried, in the wake of a verdict favorable to Burnett, to disassociate itself from such tabloids as the *Enquirer*.

Tabloid journalism uses hearsay—the anonymous source—as a method for collecting information about celebrities' private lives. Establishment newspapers are known for their reliance on eyewitness accounts and interviews with participants. But legitimate print and broadcast journalists have made mistakes of their own, some of which rival, if not surpass, the *Enquirer*'s shoddy treatment of Burnett. Increasingly, libel cases have been successfully aimed at mainstream news media, ranging from *60 Minutes* to *Time Magazine*.

Northeastern University sociologist Arnold Arluke and I tried to determine the prevalence of hearsay in legitimate front-page journalism. To this end, we examined the front page of the *New York Times* Sunday edition from October 1985 to September 1986. We found that as many as 70% of these front-page stories were unattributable. Many were so vague that they could have referred to almost anyone: "sources close to the investigation," "officials," "intelligence sources," "a key official," "critics," "campaign strategists," and the like. Some reporters even admitted to using thirdhand sources or obtaining information over the phone from an unknown person.

The reliable source has always been an important and legitimate technique of investigative journalism. (Without "Deep Throat," we might never have learned of the Watergate cover-up.) In the 1970s, unadulterated hearsay could be found in only 35% of the front-page articles published in the *New York Times*. But in the 1990s, the anonymous source became common in gathering information for front-page stories.

When *Enquirer* reporters use an anonymous source to get some "dirt" on Carol Burnett, they harm one individual. When a daily newspaper uncritically accepts the word of an anonymous source concerning an international event, it may damage the reputation of an entire country or the relationship between nations. When the *Star* bases a story about Michael Jackson on "a source close to the celebrity," we are skeptical. When the *New York Times* or the *Washington Post* relies on an off-the-record comment to develop a front-page story, we think of it as hard news. In the era of the tabloidization of news, the distinction between supermarket tabloids and legitimate daily newspapers has blurred in fact, if not yet in the public mind. ■

■ **FOCUS** *Suggestions for Further Reading*

Which came first, the chicken or the egg? In sociology, the debate is frequently between religion and the economy. For a classic account of the influence of Protestantism on capitalism, read Max Weber's *The Protestant Ethic and the Spirit of Capitalism* (1958). To examine the opposite view, that the state of the economy determines the direction of the religious institution, read Karl Marx and Frederick Engels's *On Religion* (1964).

As discussed in "The Boomerang Effect in Planning Social Change," even the best intentions sometimes go awry. Robert Merton's essay concerning unanticipated findings is found in *Social Theory and Social Structure* (1957). For a more recent discussion of the boomerang effect, read Samuel Sieber's book *Fatal Remedies* (1981).

Human intervention into the processes of social change often takes the form of collective protests. Grounded in particular cases, a recent work presents a variety of perspectives—both historical and cross cultural—on such protests as vehicles for social change. See Charles Andrain and David Apter's (1995) *Political Protest and Social Change*.

Concerning "Fads," I owe much of my analysis to Ernie Anastos's *Twixt: Teens Yesterday and Today* (1983). He provides an engrossing photo history of changing adolescent fashion, hairstyles, dances, and heroes since the 1920s. For a discussion of fashion as it relates to gender roles and aging, I also recommend Alison Lurie's readable, intriguing, and often sociological book, *The Language of Clothing* (1981). *American Fads* (1985), by Richard

Johnson, provides a description of 40 fads, from silly putty and swallowing goldfish to hot pants and Hula Hoops. For an in-depth examination of a particular fad, see Benigno E. Aguirre, E. L. Quarantelli, and Jorge L. Mendoza's (1988) "The Collective Behavior of Fads: The Characteristics, Effects, and Career of Streaking" in the August issue of the journal *American Sociological Review*.

My discussion of changing shopping mall rumors in "Riding the Rumor Mill" was based in large part on ideas developed by psychologists and sociologists over a span of 50 years. I gathered the details of particular rumors by talking with the reporters who covered the stories and by reading their newspaper accounts. Psychologists have long defined rumor as a message passed by word of mouth that becomes increasingly distorted as it travels from person to person. See Gordon Allport and Leo Postman's "The Basic Psychology of Rumor," in *Readings in Social Psychology*, edited by G. E. Swanson, T. M. Newcomb, and E. L. Hartley (1952). From a sociological point of view, however, rumor can be regarded as an informal source of news, a collective experience that the members of a group employ to define an extraordinary situation. After an earthquake hits an area, for example, you can count on the spread of rumor to fill gaps in public anxiety until official information is finally available. This sociological concept can be found in Tamotsu Shibutani's pioneering work titled *Improvised News* (1966). The link between anxiety and rumor mongering was made clear in Ralph Rosnow and Gary Fine's excellent book *Rumor and Gossip: The Social Psychology of Hearsay* (1976). For an insightful account of the spread of commercial rumors, read Fredrick Koenig's *Rumor in the Marketplace: The Social Psychology of Commercial Hearsay* (1985). Finally, Patricia A. Turner's (1993) work on rumors in African-American culture can be found in her book *I Heard It Through the Grapevine*.

"Highway to Hell?" focuses attention on the impact of technology (in this case, the automobile) in determining the direction and quality of social change. For a pop culture treatment of how the automobile is implicated in what many observers now call "road rage," see "Rudes of the Road," in the January 12, 1998 issue of *Time*.

Many theorists have emphasized the role of technological innovation, beginning with William Ogburn's (1950) classic treatment titled *Social Change*, which he originally published in 1922. To illustrate the power of technology in the process of social change, Ogburn suggested that slavery in the United States was greatly encouraged by the invention of the cotton gin in 1795. By increasing productivity and therefore profits, this single technological innovation—the gin—depended on large numbers of laborers to work the cotton fields. The plantation economy quickly dominated the southern landscape, where it remained in full force for more than 100 years.

Concerning "Enquiring Times," much of the research was taken from my work with Arnold Arluke as reported in *Gossip: The Inside Scoop* (1987). For this book, we interviewed gossip columnists and tabloid reporters and studied supermarket tabloids, popular celebrity biographies, and the front page of *The New York Times*. For an excellent treatment of the role of gossip as an agent of social control cross culturally, try Sally E. Merry's chapter "Rethinking Gossip and Scandal," in *Toward a General Theory of Social Control*, edited by Donald Black (1984). I highly recommend Robin Dunbar's (1997) fascinating book entitled *Grooming, Gossip, and the Evolution of Language*, in which the author treats gossip as an essential part of social cohesion—as the human equivalent of grooming in primates. ■

## ■ DEVELOPING IDEAS  *About Social Change*

1. Research topic: This task requires some library work. Find a best-selling magazine that has been around for several decades and contains advertisement photos featuring men and women. Take at least a couple of different time periods—for example, war versus peace time, prosperity versus recession. Examine each ad photo to determine how changes in the larger society may have influenced fashions of the day. Be sure to keep a written record of important information, such as the year, magazine title, whether the model in an ad was a man or a woman, and so on.

2. Research topic: Do a kind of sociological "family tree" that might inform you about social changes over the generations. For example, go back in your own family at least two generations, comparing yourself with your parents and your grandparents. Compare the generations on variables such as (a) last

year of school completed, (b) jobs held, (c) place of birth, (d) favorite music, (e) the racial composition of neighbors on the block while growing up, (f) attitudes toward family life, and (g) cost of a single-family home or monthly rent.

3. Writing topic: After conducting research in Exercise 2 above, write a short essay in which you discuss social changes over three generations, using your own family to illustrate.

4. Writing topic: The role of the automobile as an item of material culture in social change has been discussed. Unlike Canada and many European countries, America never developed its system of public transportation to its maximum potential. In a short essay, develop the argument, begun in the essay, that the automobile industry is largely responsible for maintaining our love affair (or should I say marriage) with the automobile, to the exclusion of alternatives such as public buses, trains, and subways.

5. Research topic: This is a project to determine changes in the importance of gossip in election campaigns. Go to the library and locate files of a daily newspaper that has been around for a few decades. Compare the front-page newspaper coverage of any presidential election campaign before 1970 versus the coverage of the 1992 or the 1996 campaign. You might want to limit yourself to reading the front page of Sunday papers beginning with the Iowa caucus or the New Hampshire primary and ending with election day. How many references do you find concerning the personal lives of the candidates? How many references do you find regarding their moral character? How have the "issues" changed? ∎

# Into the Future

One of the most important goals of sociology as a social science is to make accurate predictions. As far as the major problems of American society are concerned, William J. Wilson's *The Truly Disadvantaged* (1987) has focused squarely on the state of the black underclass. If Wilson is correct, the ranks of the permanently unemployed may continue to swell. Not that the future of poverty in America wasn't at least vaguely discernible decades ago. Daniel Bell, in 1973, was already speculating about the characteristics of postindustrial America in his book *The Coming of the Postindustrial Society: A Venture in Social Forecasting*. In the wake of welfare cutting and reversals in affirmative action legislation, some have predicted a race war in America, but it is by no means clear that such a catastrophic event will occur.

In *Forecasting Crime Data* (1978), my colleague James A. Fox provides an important example of the way in which sociologists can successfully make projections into the future based on demographic data. He correctly predicted the soaring crime rate we experienced until 1980. Then, he correctly predicted the decline through the middle 1980s. Unfortunately, no criminologist was able to foresee a sudden upswing in serious crimes beginning in the mid-1980s and continuing into the early 1990s. Then, from the mid-1990s on, the rate of serious crime took a plunge. Again, many criminologists were surprised.

So sociologists aren't psychics; we don't pretend to have perfectly clear snapshots of the future (we are doing well to come up with clear pictures of the present). Like economists and political scientists, we may be willing occasionally to take an educated guess as to the direction of society, admitting that there are too many variables to make precise predictions about almost anything. Sure, $X$ will grow, unless, of course, $Y$ suddenly declines. Sure, $A$ will improve, assuming, of course, $B$ isn't modified first. We don't always know $Y$ and $B$, so our projections about $X$ and $A$ are less than perfect. And we haven't even mentioned the assumptions we make about $C, D, E, F, G, H, I, J, K, L, M, N, O, P, Q, R, S, T, U, V, W,$ *and* $Z$—the many other important variables that influence changes in social structure and culture.

It's not just sociologists, of course, who are imperfect prognosticators. Few economists were able to predict the energy shortage that began in 1973; even fewer political scientists forecast the crumbling of the Berlin Wall or the toppling of the Soviet Union. And our 1991 Persian Gulf war seemed to come out of nowhere, as far as the literature of social science is concerned.

The leading edge of the baby boom generation will soon be well into its fifties, and their children will be approaching young adulthood. Like every other generation, the baby boomers will make plans to retire from the labor force. However, they won't feel pressured to do so. Instead, during the opening decades of the 21st century, they are likely to be offered incentives to remain in what is likely to become an ever-shrinking labor force. At this point, you can expect the typical retirement age to move from 65 to 70, or even older. Early retirement will all but disappear as an option.

Also by the first decade of the new century, the children of the baby boomers will be deeply entrenched in the crime-prone age group—late teens through early 20s (there will be a 15% increase in the number of teenagers over the next decade), and the rate of violent crime may once again soar. For the same reason, college admissions requirements are likely to become increasingly competitive. Academically marginal and older students (those often called "nontraditional" by college administrators) will have to compete against growing numbers of traditionally defined "college-aged" students—children of the baby boomers between the ages of 18 and 22. Academic "late-bloomers" are likely to lose out, as they are no longer wooed by formerly eager admissions committees.

And at the beginning and end of every century (not to mention every millennium), organized groups emerge to prophesize the end of the world. This millennial myth can be traced back to ancient Biblical writings that predict that a cosmic cataclysm orchestrated by God will destroy the ruling powers of evil and raise the righteous to a new existence in a messianic kingdom lasting 1,000 years. This is the prophesied millennium.

But, as Phil Lamy (1996) suggests in his book *Millennium Rage*, not all contemporary millennialists are sitting back and waiting for God to destroy the old system and usher in the new. Their vision of apocalypse goes far beyond any vision of a spiritual New Age metamorphosis. For some of these new apocalyptic thinkers, a declining rate of economic growth since 1970 is the result not of abstract forces such as global competition and automation, but active behind-the-scenes covert manipulation by human beings with a purpose—international bankers, the United Nations, the federal reserve system, and one-world-order types who benefit at the expense of the average American. Their notion of apocalypse is just as active and just as physical—all-out war, nothing more, nothing less.

Other apocalyptic thinkers have recently given death a helping hand. In 1994 and 1995, 69 members of a doomsday cult known as the Solar Temple perished in fires set in Canada and in Switzerland. Maybe you remember reading about it. Then, in 1997, five more members of the Solar Temple committed mass suicide in a burning house in Quebec.

On March 26, 1997, 39 members of the Heaven's Gate cult committed mass suicide in their rented mansion in Rancho Santa Fe near San Diego. Marshall Applewhite, the cult's leader, had convinced his followers—20 women and 19 men ranging in age from 26 to 72—that a spaceship traveling behind the Hale-Bopp comet was coming to pick them all up soon after they had shed their "vehicles" or "containers" (also known as bodies). They were totally convinced that civilization on Earth was about to end, but that they could enter a higher plane of life by getting rid of their bodies and boarding a spaceship from what they called the next level.

If the passage to the next millennium is anything like previous transitions, we are sure to see, in the years ahead, even more deadly forms of apocalyptic behavior. Yet, most aging baby boomers will be very little affected, in any personal sense, by the new calendar. Instead, they will continue to be like every generation to precede them by reducing their spending and their use of credit cards. As they actually begin to retire from the labor force, the boomers will, as a result, finally forfeit their cultural clout as well. Just as members of the "twentysomething" generation presently feel they are playing second fiddle to the boomers, so more and more young Americans in the future will resent the presence of huge numbers of retired Guppies (gray urban professionals) who live on their Social Security checks and require expensive health care insurance to survive.

By the early decades of the new millennium, multiculturalism will become a focal point of social change. Growing numbers of immigrants and minorities—African, Asian, and Latin American—will ensure that the white Anglo-Saxon majority is no longer the majority. In our postindustrial society, there will be growing conflict between groups for scarce economic resources.

In their recent effort *The Good Society* (1991), Robert Bellah, Richard Madsen, William Sullivan, Ann Swidler, and Steven Tipton argue that we can solve our growing social problems by transforming our institutions—our schools, family, corporations, church, and state. As they so eloquently did in *Habits of the Heart* (1985), Bellah et al. decry the rise of raw individualism in American society. Calling for public debate concerning our social ills, they propose a blueprint for the future of American society. In *The Good Society*, they assert that we are fully capable of making changes in our values and of taking responsibility for our economic and political institutions.

The technological outlook may be even rosier, according to Gene Bylinski. In an article in *Fortune* titled "Technology in the Year 2000" (1988), he is sanguine regarding our ability to employ future technological discoveries to heal the human body and help us to live fuller lives. Arguably, the most innovative period in our history occurred during the transition into the 20th century. Roughly between 1870 and 1930, we saw the invention of the automobile, telephone, light bulb, airplane, phonograph, radio, and motion picture. Later in the century, we witnessed the introduction of personal computers as well as certain medical advances (e.g., antibiotics) that have had a major impact on our daily lives. Other important inventions of the century included the transistor, the silicon chip, faxes and copiers, air conditioning, plastics, the compact disc, television, jet planes, radar, and the birth-control pill. Of course, the 20th century also left us with nuclear weapons.

In the years ahead, we will be left to make a number of important decisions concerning the uses of technological advances. For example, will our growing sophistication in the area of rocketry be used to explore the universe or to blow ourselves into smithereens? Will our increasing reliance on personal computers and CD-ROMs produce shorter workweeks and higher incomes or more severe income inequality between educated specialists and the remaining low-skilled, low-paid workforce? Will future medical advances be employed to increase the quality of our lives or will growing numbers of Americans live to a ripe old age, only to exist in an unproductive, vegetative state? We can speculate as to where we are headed, but only time will tell for certain (McGinn & Raymond, 1998).

Sociology has often been regarded as subversive. In a sense, it is. That is to say, sociologists often challenge our taken-for-granted assumptions, the status quo, and, more precisely, the people in charge of things. No wonder totalitarian societies rarely permit their college students to study the field of sociology, or, when they do, they keep it under rigid controls. For the same reason, even in societies that permit greater freedom of choice, sociologists aren't always welcome or appreciated. They might rock the political boat. They might advocate expensive programs and policies. Their research might be useful to reformists who agitate for social change.

The importance of the field of sociology—or more precisely, the collective respect for it—varies according to the urgency of our social problems and the extent of our prosperity as a society. In popular culture terms, we have to believe that we *need* sociologists, but we also have to feel we can *afford* them. The "hip generation" of the 1960s and early 1970s, for example, was a heyday for the field. By 1973, the number of college students earning their bachelor's degrees in sociology had reached a record high of 35,996. Inflation was relatively low, the economy was growing, and there were several important social issues to inspire interest. Civil rights, feminism, and war were on almost everybody's mind. Our inner cities were burning while thousands marched through the streets to protest, demonstrate, or riot. As a result, millions looked to social scientists to give them advice about how to run society, how to solve the urgent problems of the day. Not that anyone in charge often implemented the answers that sociologists provided, but at least we were asked.

In the February 3, 1992 issue of *Newsweek*, reporter Barbara Kantrowitz, in her article "Sociology's Lonely Crowd," summarizes some of the problems and prospects of the discipline. She reports that by 1989, the number of students receiving bachelor's degrees in sociology had dwindled to only 14,393. Long holding a reputation as being among the more liberal of the arts and sciences, sociology apparently did not fit very well into the cultural milieu of the 1980s. Students turned to majors such as business and engineering, which they considered to be more "practical." Moreover, many undergraduates enrolled in specialized professional programs—criminal justice, social work, urban studies, and market research—which began in and are actually offshoots of sociology.

In the last few years, however, we have seen a reversal of this trend. Enrollment in sociology courses is again on the rise, as growing numbers of undergraduates recognize that sociological training is connected to a range of attractive career paths—from doing significant work in a federal agency to running a successful consulting business (Levine, 1997). Moreover, we are just beginning to recognize the need to address growing social problems such as homelessness, crime, and poverty. The black underclass is much larger today than it was in the 1960s when civil disorder enveloped our major cities in flames. Kids are murdering one another at ever-younger ages. If present trends continue unabated, it is safe to predict that sociologists will gain prominence in the next century. The United States continues to struggle with long-standing problems that reduce our quality of life and frustrate our collective aspirations. Finding effective solutions will require that we put aside our differences and pull together as a society. We can only hope that Americans will rise to the challenge. ∎

# Bibliography

Aguirre, Benigno E., Quarantelli, E. L., & Mendoza, Jorge L. (1988, August). The collective behavior of fads: the characteristics, effects, and career of streaking. *American Sociological Review.*

Allport, Gordon, & Postman, Leo (1952). The basic psychology of rumor. In G. E. Swanson, T. M. Newcomb, & E. L. Hartley (Eds.), *Readings in social psychology.* New York: Holt.

Anastos, Ernie (1983). *Twixt: Teens yesterday and today.* New York: Franklin Watts.

Andrain, Charles F., & Apter, David E. (1995). *Political protest and social change.* New York: New York University.

Archer, Dane, & Gartner, Rosemary (1984). *Violence and crime in cross-national perspective.* New Haven, CT: Yale University Press.

Arluke, Arnold & Sanders, Clinton R. (1996). *Regarding animals.* Philadelphia: Temple University Press.

Asch, Solomon (1952). Effects of group pressure upon the modification and distortion of judgment. In G. E. Swanson (Ed.), *Readings in social psychology.* New York: Rinehart & Winston.

Ball-Rokeach, Sandra, & Cantor, Muriel (1986). *Media, audience, and social structure.* Beverly Hills, CA: Sage.

Barcus, F. Earle (1983). *Images of life on children's television: Sex roles, minorities, and families.* New York: Praeger.

Barnett, Rosalind C. (1994, August). Home-to-work spillover revisited: A study of full-time employed women in dual-earner couples. *Journal of Marriage and the Family.*

Bateson, Mary Catherine (1990). *Composing a life.* New York: Plume.

Becker, Howard S. (1967). Whose side are we on? *Social Problems, 14,* 239-247.

Becker, Howard S., Geer, Blanche, Hughes, Everett C., & Strauss, Amselm L. (1961). *Boys in white.* Chicago: University of Chicago Press.

Bell, Daniel (1973). *The coming of the postindustrial society: A venture in social forecasting.* New York: Basic Books.

Bellah, Robert, Madsen, Richard, Sullivan, William, Swidler, Ann, & Tipton, Steven (1985). *Habits of the heart: Individualism and commitment in American life.* Berkeley: University of California Press.

Bellah, Robert, Madsen, Richard, Sullivan, William, Swidler, Ann, & Tipton, Steven (1991). *The good society.* New York: Knopf.

Blumstein, Alfred (1995, August). Violence by young people: Why the deadly nexus? *National Institute of Justice Journal,* 2-9.

Bowers, William J. (1974). *Executions in America.* Lexington, MA: Lexington Books.

Bowers, William J. (1984). *Legal homicide: Death as punishment in America, 1864–1982.* With Glenn L. Pierce and John F. McDevitt. Boston: Northeastern University.

Breines, Winifred (1992). *Young, white, and miserable: Growing up female in the fifties.* Boston: Beacon.

Butler, Robert (1975). *Why survive? Being old in America.* New York: Harper & Row.

Bylinski, Gene (1988, July 18). Technology in the year 2000. *Fortune*, 65-68.

Cantor, Muriel, & Pingree, Susanne (1983). *The soap opera*. Beverly Hills, CA: Sage.
Chernin, Kim (1981). *The obsession: Reflections on the tyranny of slenderness*. New York: Harper & Row.
Chudacoff, Howard (1989). *How old are you?* Princeton, NJ: Princeton University Press.
Comer, James P. (1972). *Beyond black and white*. Chicago: Quadrangle.
Comstock, Gary D. (1991). *Violence against lesbians and gay men*. New York: Columbia University Press.
Cooley, Charles H. (1902). *Human nature and the social order*. New York: Scribner.
Coser, Lewis (1956). *The functions of social conflict*. New York: Free Press.

Davis, Kingsley, & Moore, Wilbert (1945). Some principles of stratification. *American Sociological Review, 10*, 242-249.
Dunbar, Robin (1997). *Grooming, gossip, and the evolution of language*. Cambridge, MA: Harvard University.
Durkheim, Émile (1933). *The division of labor in society*. New York: Free Press.
Durkheim, Émile (1951). *Suicide: A study in sociology*. New York: Free Press.
Durkheim, Émile (1966). *The rules of sociological method*. New York: Free Press.

Ebaugh, Helen Rose Fuchs (1988). *Becoming an ex: The process of role exit*. Chicago: University of Chicago.
Ehrlich, Howard J. (1990). *Campus ethnoviolence and the policy options*. Baltimore, MD: National Institute Against Prejudice and Violence.
Erikson, Eric H. (1950). *Childhood and society*. New York: Norton.

Fowler, Rebekah I., & Fuehrer, Ann (1997). Women's marital names: An interpretive study of name retainers' concepts of marriage. *Feminism and Psychology, 7*(3), 315-320.
Fox, James A. (1978). *Forecasting crime data*. Lexington, MA: Lexington Books.
Fox, James A. (1996, March). *Trends in juvenile violence*. A report to the U.S. Attorney General for the Bureau of Justice Statistics on "Current and Future Rates of Juvenile Offending," Northeastern University.
Fox, James A., & Levin, Jack (1994). *Overkill: Mass murder and serial killing exposed*. New York: Plenum.

Gans, Herbert J. (1972). The positive functions of poverty. *American Journal of Sociology, 78*, 275-289.
Gerbner, George, Gross, Larry, Morgan, Michael, & Signorielli, Nancy (1982). Charting the mainstream: Television's contributions to political orientations. *Journal of Communication, 32*, 100-127.
Gerth, H. H., & Mills, C. Wright (Eds.). (1946). *Max Weber: Essays in sociology*. New York: Oxford University Press.
Glazer, Myron Peretz, & Glazer, Penina Migdal (1989). *The whistleblowers: Exposing corruption in government and industry*. New York: Basic Books.
Goffman, Erving (1958). *Asylums*. New York: Anchor.

Goffman, Erving (1963). *Stigma: Notes on the management of spoiled identity.* Englewood Cliffs, NJ: Prentice Hall.
Gottfredson, Michael, & Hirschi, Travis (1990). *A general theory of crime.* Stanford, CA: Stanford University Press.
Gowen, Teresa (1998). American untouchables: Homeless scavengers in San Francisco's underground economy. In Amy Wharton (Ed.). *Working in America: Continuity, conflict, and change.* Mountain View, CA: Mayfield.
Granfield, Robert (1986). Legal education as corporate ideology. *Sociological Forum, 1,* 514-523.

Harris, Marvin (1979). *Cultural materialism.* New York: Random House.
Herek, Gregory, & Berrill, Kevin (Eds.). (1992). *Hate crimes: Confronting violence against lesbians and gay men.* Newbury Park, CA: Sage.
Hoffman, Bill, & Burke, Cathy (1997). *Heaven's Gate.* New York: Harper Paperbacks.
Hughes, Everett (1962). Good people and dirty work. *Social Problems, 10,* 3-11.

Johnson, Richard (1985). *American fads.* New York: Beech Tree.
Jones, Landon Y. (1980). *Great expectations: America and the baby boom generation.* New York: Ballantine.

Kalberg, Stephen (1980). Max Weber's types of rationality: Cornerstones for the analysis of *rationalization* processes in history. *American Journal of Sociology, 85,* 1145-1179.
Kanter, Rosabeth M. (1993). *Men and women of the corporation* (2nd ed.). New York: Basic Books.
Kantrowitz, Barbara (1992, February 3). Sociology's lonely crowd. *Newsweek,* 22-28.
Karl, Jonathan (1995). *The right to bear arms.* New York: HarperPaperbacks.
Katz, Jack (1988). *Seductions of crime: Moral and sensual attractions of doing evil.* New York: Basic Books.
Kaufman, Debra Renee (1991). *Rachel's daughters.* New Brunswick, NJ: Rutgers University Press.
Keen, Sam (1986). *Faces of the enemy: Reflections of the hostile imagination.* San Francisco: Harper & Row.
Kennedy, Daniel, & Kerber, August (1973). *Resocialization: An American experiment.* New York: Behavioral Publications.
Koenig, Fredrick (1985). *Rumor in the marketplace: The social psychology of commercial hearsay.* Dover, MA: Auburn House.
Kohn, Alfie (1990). *The brighter side of human nature.* New York: Basic Books.
Kollock, Peter, & O'Brien, Jodi (1994). *The production of reality.* Thousand Oaks, CA: Pine Forge.
Kuhn, Manford (1960). Self-attitudes by age, sex, and professional training. *Sociological Quarterly, 1,* 39-55.

Lamy, Philip (1996). *Millennium rage.* New York: Plenum.
Largey, Gale, & Watson, David (1972). The sociology of odors. *American Journal of Sociology, 77,* 1021-1034.
Larson, Mary Strom (1996, July). Sex roles and soap operas. *Sex Roles, 22,* 281-287.

Leinberger, Paul, & Tucker, Bruce (1991). *The new individualists: the generation after the organization man.* New York: HarperCollins.
Levin, Jack (1993). Misery as a turning point for academic success. *Journal of Research in Education, 3,* 3-6.
Levin, Jack (1998). Violence goes to school. *Mid-Western Educational Researcher, 11,* 2-7.
Levin, Jack, & Arluke, Arnold (1987). *Gossip: The inside scoop.* New York: Plenum.
Levin, Jack, Arluke, Arnold, & Levin, William C. (1992, August). Powerful elders. Paper presented at the annual meeting of the American Sociological Association, New York.
Levin, Jack, & Fox, James A. (1991). *Mass murder: America's growing menace.* New York: Berkley.
Levin, Jack, & Levin, William C. (1980). *Ageism: Prejudice and discrimination against the elderly.* Belmont, CA: Wadsworth.
Levin, Jack, & Levin, William C. (1982). *The functions of discrimination and prejudice* (2nd ed.). New York: Harper & Row.
Levin, Jack, & Levin, William C. (1991). Sociology of educational late-blooming. *Sociological Forum, 6,* 661-680.
Levin, Jack, & McDevitt, Jack (1993). *Hate crimes: The rising tide of bigotry and bloodshed.* New York: Plenum.
Levin, William C. (1988). Age stereotyping: College student evaluations. *Research on Aging, 10,* 134-148.
Levine, Robert (1997). The pace of life in 31 countries. *American Demographics,* November.
Lorenz, Konrad (1966). *On aggression.* New York: Harcourt Brace.
Lowenthal, Leo (1961). *Literature, popular culture and society.* New York: Prentice Hall.
Lurie, Alison (1981). *The language of clothing.* New York: Random House.
Lynd, Robert S., & Lynd, Helen M. (1929). *Middletown: A study in American culture.* New York: Harcourt Brace.

MacDonald, John M. (1968). *Homicidal threats.* Springfield, IL: Charles C Thomas.
MacManus, Susan A. (1996). *Young vs. old: Generational combat in the 21st century.* Boulder, CO: Westview.
Madrick, Jeffrey (1995). *The end of affluence.* New York: Random House.
Maguire, Kathleen, & Pastore, Ann L. (1996). *Bureau of Justice statistics sourcebook of criminal justice statistics—1995.* Washington, DC: U.S. Government Printing Office.
Marx, Karl (1967). *Das kapital.* New York: International. (Original work published 1867-1895)
Marx, Karl, & Engels, Frederick (1964). "On religion." In T. B. Bottomore and Maximillian Rubel (Eds.), *Selected writings in sociology and social philosophy.* Baltimore, MD: Penguin. (Original work published 1848)
McGinn, Daniel, & Raymond, Joan (1998, February 9). [Special Issue]. *Newsweek,* 32-33.
Mead, George Herbert (1934). *Mind, self and society.* Chicago: University of Chicago Press.
Mecca, Andrew, Smelser, Neil, & Vasconcellos, John (Eds.). (1989). *The social importance of self-esteem.* Berkeley: University of California Press.
Merry, Sally E. (1984). Rethinking gossip and scandal. In Donald Black (Ed.), *Toward a general theory of social control.* Orlando, FL: Academic Press.
Merton, Robert K. (1957). *Social theory and social structure.* Glencoe, IL: Free Press.
Milgram, Stanley (1974). *Obedience to authority: An experimental view.* New York: Harper & Row.
Millman, Marcia (1980). *Such a pretty face.* New York: Simon & Schuster.

Mirowsky, John, & Ross, Catherine (1989). *Social causes of psychological distress.* New York: Aldine de Gruyter.

Newman, Katherine (1988). *Falling from grace: The experience of downward mobility in the American middle class.* New York: Free Press.

Noguera, P. A. (1995). Preventing and producing violence: A critical analysis of responses to school violence. *Harvard Educational Review, Summer,* 189-212.

Ogburn, William F. (1950). *Social change.* New York: Viking. (Original work published 1922)

Oliner, Samuel, & Oliner, Pearl (1988). *The altruistic personality.* New York: Free Press.

Oliver, Melvin L., & Shapiro, Thomas M. (n.d.). *Black wealth/white wealth.* New York: Routledge.

Orbach, Susie (1978). *Fat is a feminist issue.* New York: Paddington.

Phillips, Kevin (1990). *The politics of the rich and the poor.* New York: Random House.

Portes, Alejandro, & Rumbaut, Ruben G. (1990). *Immigrant America: A portrait.* Berkeley: University of California Press.

Radelet, Michael L., Bedau, Hugo Adam, & Putnam, Constance E. (1992). *In spite of innocence.* Boston: Northeastern University Press.

Reiman, Jeffrey (1989). *The rich get richer and the poor get prison* (3rd ed.). New York: John Wiley.

Riesman, David (1950). *The lonely crowd.* New Haven, CT: Yale University Press.

Ritzer, George (1993). *The McDonaldization of society.* Newbury Park, CA: Pine Forge.

Ritzer, George (1995). *Expressing America.* Thousand Oaks, CA: Pine Forge.

Rose, Arnold (1962). Reactions against the mass society. *Sociological Quarterly, 3,* 310-319.

Rosenhan, David (1973). On being sane in insane places. *Science, 179,* 250-258.

Rosenthal, Robert, & Jacobson, Lenore (1968). *Pygmalion in the classroom.* New York: Holt.

Rosnow, Ralph, & Fine, Gary (1976). *Rumor and gossip: The social psychology of hearsay.* New York: Elsevier.

Rowan, Carl T. (1996). *The coming race war in America.* Boston: Little, Brown.

Rudes of the Road (1998, January 12). *Time Magazine.*

Sampson, Robert, & Laub, John (1994). *Crime in the making: Pathways and turning points through life.* Cambridge, MA: Harvard University Press.

Schabas, William A. (1997). *The international sourcebook on capital punishment.* Boston: Northeastern University Press.

Shibutani, Tamotsu (1966). *Improvised news.* Indianapolis, IN: Bobbs-Merrill.

Sidel, Ruth (1994). *Battling bias.* New York: Penguin.

Sieber, Samuel (1981). *Fatal remedies.* New York: Plenum.

Singer, Margaret Thaler (1995). *Cults in our midst: The hidden menace in our everyday lives.* San Francisco: Jossey-Bass.

Smolla, Rodney A. (1986). *Suing the press.* New York: Oxford University Press.

Tabor, James, & Gallagher, Eugene (1995). *Why Waco? Cults and the battle for religious freedom in America.* Berkeley: University of California Press.
Tumin, Melvin (1953). Some principles of stratification: A critical analysis. *American Sociological Review, 18,* 387-394.
Turner, Patricia A. (1993). *I heard it through the grapevine.* Berkeley: University of California Press.

Weber, Max (1958). *The Protestant ethic and the spirit of capitalism.* New York: Scribner's.
Whyte, William H. (1956). *The organization man.* New York: Simon & Schuster.
Wilson, William J. (1987). *The truly disadvantaged.* Chicago: University of Chicago Press.
Wright, Charles, R. (1986). *Mass communication: A sociological perspective.* New York: Random House.

Zimbardo, Philip C., Haney, Craig, & Banks, William C. (1973, April 8). A Pirandellian prison. *New York Times Magazine.*
Zurubavel, Eviatar (1981). *Hidden rhythms: Schedules and calendars in social life.* Chicago: University of Chicago Press.

# Index

Activism, idols of, 40, 46
Adulthood:
    criminality, 74-75
    socialization in, 70-71
    *See also* Elder population
Affirmative action, 161
Altruism, 38-40, 47
Anger, age of, 162
Animal cruelty, 135-136, 139-140
Anomie, state of, 8-9, 17-18, 19
Asch, Solomon, 45
Automobiles in America, 185-187

Baby boomers:
    aging, 35-36
    cultural clout, 34-35, 46, 48
    future of, 198
    music of, 33-34
Bathing:
    American culture, 30, 31, 46
    group differences, 31-32
    historically, 30-31
Becker, Howard, 123
Boomerang Effect, 172-173, 175-177, 191
Bureaucracy, 92-94, 95-96
Bystander apathy, 37-38

Capital punishment, 122-123, 131-132, 139
    deterrence, 132-133
    prisoner maintenance, 132
    revenge, 131, 134
    societal protection, 133
Census Bureau, 18
Changes in society. *See* Social change
Children/teenagers:
    attitudes toward, 48
    fads, 178-180
    hate crimes, 137-138, 140
    of organization men, 93-94, 95-96
    violence by, 42-43, 47, 65-66, 74, 104-105
Community:
    eclipse of, 109
    *See also* Individualism vs. community
Conformity, 45
Cooley, Charles Horton, 55
Crime, violent, 41-42, 42-43, 59-60
Cults, 86-88, 95
Cultural content, 28, 53
    economics, influence of, 26-27
    heroes in, 27-28, 40, 46, 47-48
    stereotypes, 55-56
Cultural diffusion, 26
Cultural revolution:
    smoking, 42
    teenagers in, 42
    violent crime, 41-42, 42-43

Death Penalty. *See* Capital punishment
Deviance, 121-124
    American automobile, 185-186
    animal cruelty/human violence, 135-136, 139-140
    death penalty, 131-134
    developing ideas about, 141-143
    mental health institutions, 129-130, 141
    obesity, 125-128, 140-141
    predicting, 123-124
    scapegoating/hate crimes, 137-138, 149
Domestic violence, 59-60
Downward mobility, 150-151, 163
Durkheim, Emile, 122, 139

Einstein exemption, 159
Elder population, 153-154, 164
Elevator culture, 44-45
Erikson, Eric, 70, 71

Family, 104-105, 114

Gans, Herbert, 112-113
Goffman, Erving, 121, 122, 129
Gold rush fever, 17
Good Samaritans, 38, 39-40
Groups, 81-83
    bureaucratic organizations, 92-94, 95-96
    cults, 86-88, 95
    developing ideas about, 96-97
    fraternities/sororities, 84-85
    mass societies, 84, 85, 95
    recommuning/reunions, 89-91, 95

Hawthorne Effect, 42
Heartburn, 16-18, 19
Heroes, 27-28, 40, 46, 47-48

Idols of activism. *See* Heroes
Immigration Act of 1990, 159
Immigration. *See* Social inequality
Individualism vs. community, 47
    bureaucratic organizations, 92-94, 95-96
    mass societies, 84, 85, 95
    *See also* Institutions
Inequality. *See* Social inequality
Institutions, 101-103
    developing ideas about, 115-116
    dirty work, 111-113, 115
    formal systems of care, 106-107, 114
    marginalized social solutions, 108-110, 114-115
    mental health, 129-130, 141
    moral authority of, 104-105, 114

Late bloomers, 12-15, 19
Life chances, 147-148
Lowenthal, Leo, 27

Marginalization of America, 108-110
Marx, Karl, 27, 171, 172
Mass societies, 84
Migrant workers, 17, 18
Milennialism, 198-199

NAAFA. *See* National Association to Aid Fat Americans
Names:
    disabilities, 68
    given, 67-68, 69, 72
    minorities, 68
National Association to Aid Fat Americans, 127-128
National Rolaids Heartburn Index, 16

Obesity, 125-128, 140-141
Occupations, specialized, 111-113

Patriot Movement, 155-157, 164

Race in America, 161-163, 165
Responsibility, diffusion of, 37
Reunions, 89-91, 95
Roles, 7, 18
    bureaucratic organizations, 92-94, 95-96
    power of, 10-11
    role taking, 72
Rumors, 181-182
    Entenmann's bakery, 182-183
    shopping malls, dangers of, 183-184
    sburbia, 182

Scapegoating, 137-138, 149
School:
    socialization, 54
    violence in, 65-66, 74
Segregation, 55
Self-concept, 129
Self-esteem, 55-56
    cults, 87-88, 95
    labeling, 72
    social problems, 72-73
    *See also* Names; Obesity
Self-ethic, 93-94
Serial killers, 70-71, 121
Smoking, 42
Social change, 171-174
    and the automobile, 187, 192-193
    Boomerang Effect, 172-173, 175-177, 191
    developing ideas about, 193-194
    evolution, 172

fads, 178-180, 191-192
millennialism, 198-199
rumors and, 181-184, 192
tabloidization of news, 188-191, 193
technological discoveries, 200
Social inequality, 147-149
   developing ideas about, 166-167
   downward mobility/economic escalator, 150-151, 163
   economic system, injustices of, 165
   elderly, status of, 153-154, 164
   immigration, 158-160, 164-165
   life chances, 147-148
   Patriot Movement, 155-157, 164
   race in America, 161-163, 165
   stratification, 147, 151, 163-164
Social structure, 19-20
   bureaucratic organizations, 92-94, 95-96
   developing ideas about, 20-21
   mass societies, 84, 85, 95
   *See also* Roles; Institutions
Socialization, 53-54
   adulthood, 70-71
   cultural stereotypes, 55-56, 57-60
   developing ideas about, 75-77
   looking glass process, 55
   mass media, 54-55
   mental health institutions and, 129-130
   school and, 54
   soap operas and, 61-62
   subcultural identification, 55
Sociology, 6-7, 201-202
   advocacy, 123
   anomie, state of, 8-9, 17-18, 19
   opportunity, 8, 13
   predictions, 197-198
   value free, 5-6, 122-123, 139
Sociopaths, 53
Sorokin, Pitirim, 171, 172
Spencer, Herbert, 171, 172
Stereotypes, 57
   bias in reality, 73-74
   community service, 58-59
   of the elderly, 153-154
   television and, 57-58
Stratification. *See* Social inequality

Teenagers. *See* Children/teenagers
Television, 54-55, 57-58
   soap operas, 61-64, 74

Values, 5-6, 48, 122
Violence, 41-42, 42-43, 59-60
   animal abuse, 135-136, 139-140
   city schools, 65-66

Weber, Max, 5-6, 139, 147
Whyte, William H., 92

Zimbardo, Philip, 10-11